Salutations
Greetings

When people meet, they shake hands.

When two young people meet, they say . . . **Salut!**

When two older people greet each other, they say . . .
Bonjour!

One addresses a man as . . . **monsieur,**
a married lady as . . . **madame,**
and an unmarried lady as . . . **mademoiselle.**

Time of day affects greetings as well.

In the morning, the greeting is . . . **Bonjour!**

In the evening, the greeting is . . . **Bonsoir!**

Salutations

Greet each of the following people in French.

1. your best friend ___Salut___
2. your teacher ___Bonjour___
3. your dad's boss ___Bonjour, Monsieur___
4. your principal ___Bonjour___
5. an unmarried lady ___Bonjour Mademoiselle___
6. the mailman ___Bonjour___

Write the French words that are missing.

Salut

Bonjour

Madame

Bonsoir

Bonjour Madame

Bonjour

Comment ça va?
How are you?

Nom _____

Écrivez en français.

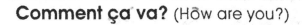

Comment ça va? (How are you?)

_____

Très bien, merci. (Very well, thanks.)

_____

Ça va bien. (Fine, thanks.)

_____

Comme ci comme ça. (So-so.)

_____

Mal. (Badly.)

_____

Très mal! (Very badly!)

_____

Comment ça va?

Nom_____

Define the following terms.

Comment ça va? _____ *How are you* _____

Ça va bien. _____ *I am well* _____

Mal! _____ *Badly!* _____

Comme ci comme ça. _____ *So - So* _____

Très bien. _____ *Very well* _____

Très mal. _____ *Very badly* _____

Answer according to the pictures.

_____ *Très bien* _____

_____ *Mal* _____

_____ *Ça va bien* _____

_____ *Comme si comme ça* _____

_____ *Très Mal* _____

4

Révision
Review

Finissez les phrases. (Complete with the appropriate words.)

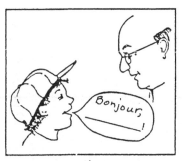
comment allez vous

Bien. Comment

c'comme ca ?

B Salut

ca va ?

bien

Bonsoir

Comment

Très

Madame

Comment ca va ?

Bien

Au revoir
Good-bye

Écrivez en français.

Au revoir. (Good-bye.)

_____

Adieu. (Formal goodbye.)

_____

À tout à l'heure. (See you later.)

_____

À demain. (See you tomorrow.)

_____

Écrivez en anglais. (Write what they are saying in English.)

Hi André

How are you

I'm well, thanks

Bye — See You later

Good bye

Comment t'appelles-tu?

What's your name?

Nom _____

In French there are two ways to ask "What's your name?" **Comment vous appelez-vous?** is more formal. It uses the word **vous**, a polite form of the word "you." **Vous** is usually used with someone you don't know very well or who is older than you.

The second way, **Comment t'appelles-tu?**, is less formal. It uses the word **tu**, a familiar form of the word "you." **Tu** is usually used with someone you know very well (a family member or close friend), someone younger than you, or a pet.

The answer, **Je m'appelle . . .** (My name . . .) is used to answer both styles of questions.

Écrivez en français.

Comment vous appelez-vous?

_____

Je m'appelle . . .

_____

Comment t'appelles-tu?

_____

Je m'appelle . . .

_____

Finissez les phrases. (Complete the sentences.)

Je m'appelle Christine. Comment t'_____, _____ ?

_____ 'appelle Pierre.

Je _____ Madame Payot. Comment vous _____ ?

_____ Monsieur Portalis.

Je m'appelle Marie-Claire. Comment _____ tu?

Je m'appelle _____ .

Révision
Review

I. Write the French words to complete the dialogues.

_____ _____ _____

_____ _____ _____

II. Greet the people below in French.

_____ _____ _____ _____

III. Now tell them each good-bye in different ways.

_____ _____ _____

_____ _____

Les nombres
Numbers

Écrivez les nombres en français.

1	2	3
un	deux	trois

4	5	6
quatre	cinq	six

7	8	9
sept	huit	neuf

10	11	12
dix	onze	douze

13	14	15
treize	quatorze	quinze

16	17	18
seize	dix-sept	dix-huit

19	20	21
dix-neuf	vingt	vingt et un

22	23	24
vingt-deux	vingt-trois	vingt-quatre

25	26	27
vingt-cinq	vingt-six	vingt-sept

28	29	30
vingt-huit	vingt-neuf	trente

Les nombres

Écrivez les nombres en français.

31
trente et un
_____

32
trente-deux
_____

33
trente-trois
_____

34
trente-quatre
_____

35
trente-cinq
_____

36
trente-six
_____

37
trente-sept
_____

38
trente-huit
_____

39
trente-neuf
_____

40
quarante
_____

41
quarante et un
_____

42
quarante-deux
_____

43
quarante-trois
_____

44
quarante-quatre
_____

45
quarante-cinq
_____

46
quarante-six
_____

47
quarante-sept
_____

48
quarante-huit
_____

49
quarante-neuf
_____

50
cinquante
_____

51
cinquante et un
_____

52
cinquante-deux
_____

53
cinquante-trois
_____

54
cinquante-quatre
_____

55
cinquante-cinq
_____

56
cinquante-six
_____

57
cinquante-sept
_____

58
cinquante-huit
_____

59
cinquante-neuf
_____

60
soixante
_____

Les nombres

Écrivez les nombres en français.

61 **soixante et un**

62 **soixante-deux**

63 **soixante-trois**

64 **soixante-quatre**

65 **soixante-cinq**

66 **soixante-six**

67 **soixante-sept**

68 **soixante-huit**

69 **soixante-neuf**

70 **soixante-dix**

71 **soixante et onze**

72 **soixante-douze**

73 **soixante-treize**

74 **soixante-quatorze**

75 **soixante-quinze**

76 **soixante-seize**

77 **soixante-dix-sept**

78 **soixante-dix-huit**

79 **soixante-dix-neuf**

80 **quatre-vingt**

81 **quatre-vingt et un**

82 **quatre-vingt-deux**

83 **quatre-vingt-trois**

84 **quatre-vingt-quatre**

85 **quatre-vingt-cinq**

86 **quatre-vingt-six**

87 **quatre-vingt-sept**

88 **quatre-vingt-huit**

89 **quatre-vingt-neuf**

90 **quatre-vingt-dix**

Les nombres

91	92	93
quatre-vingt-onze	quatre-vingt-douze	quatre-vingt-treize
94	95	96
quatre-vingt-quatorze	quatre-vingt-quinze	quatre-vingt-seize
97	98	99
quatre-vingt-dix-sept	quatre-vingt-dix-huit	quatre-vingt-dix-neuf
100	101	200
cent	cent un	deux cents
202	300	303
deux cent deux	trois cents	trois cent trois
400	404	500
quatre cents	quatre cent quatre	cinq cents
600	700	800
six cents	sept cents	huit cents
900	1,000	1,100
neuf cents	mille	mille cent
1,500	2,000	10,000
mille cinq cents	deux mille	dix mille
100,000	1,000,000	1,000,000,000
cent mille	un million	un milliard

Les nombres

Nom _____

Écrivez les nombres en français.

1. 67 _Soixante - sept_

2. 181 _cent - quatre - vingt_

3. 92 _Quatre-vingt deux et un_

4. 74 _soixante - quatorze_

5. 243 _deux cent quatorze trois_

6. 515 _____

7. 926 _____

8. 304 _____

9. 1,200 _____

10. 4,000 _____

11. 500,126 _____

12. 1,894,037 _____

13. 3,600,012 _____

14. 987,651 _____

Écrivez les nombres.

1. trois cent quatre-vingt-treize _393_

2. quarante-huit _48_

3. huit mille sept _8007_

4. mille cent un _1,101_

5. sept cent treize _____

6. deux mille onze _____

7. un million quatorze _____

8. quatre-vingt deux _____

9. cinquante _____

10. quinze mille _____

11. mille neuf cent _____

12. trois mille _____

13. deux cent seize _____

14. trois milliards _____

Write how you would say the following years in French.

exemple: 1995 mille neuf cent quatre-vingt-quinze

1492 _____

1776 _____

1955 _____

1812 _____

1548 _____

1637 _____

Les jours de la semaine
Days of the Week

Nom_____

lundi	mardi	mercredi	jeudi	vendredi	samedi	dimanche
	1	2	3	4	5	6
7	8	9	10	11	12	13
14	15	16	17	18	19	20
21	22	23	24	25	26	27
28	29	30	31			

Écrivez en français.

lundi
(Monday)

mardi
(Tuesday)

mercredi
(Wednesday)

jeudi
(Thursday)

_____

_____

_____

_____

vendredi
(Friday)

samedi
(Saturday)

dimanche
(Sunday)

le jour
(day)

_____

_____

_____

_____

I. Écrivez les jours de la semaine. (**Note:** In French Monday comes first.)

lundi, mardi, mercredi, jeudi, vendredi
samedi, dimanche

II. Écrivez le jour suivant.
   (Write the following day.)

mardi _____ mercredi

dimanche _____ lundi

jeudi _____ vendredi

lundi _____ mardi

vendredi _____ samedi

samedi _____ dimance

mercredi _____ jeudi

III. Écrivez en français.
   (Write in French.)

Sunday _____ dimanche

Tuesday _____ mardi

Wednesday _____ mercredi

Monday _____ lundi

Friday _____ vendredi

Thursday _____ jeudi

Saturday _____ samedi

Les mois
Months of the Year

Nom _____

Écrivez les mois en français.

janvier	mai	septembre
janvier	_mai_	_septembre_

février	juin	octobre
février	_juin_	_octobre_

mars	juillet	novembre
mars	_juillet_	_novembre_

avril	août	décembre
avril	_août_	_décembre_

I. Écrivez le mois suivant. (Write the following month.)

mars _avril_   janvier _février_

décembre _janvier_   avril _mai_

juillet _août_   août _septembre_

octobre _novembre_   mai _juin_

février _mars_   septembre _octobre_

juin _~~juillt~~ /juillet_   novembre _décembre_

II. Combien de jours y a-t-il dans chaque mois? Écrivez les nombres en français. (How many days are in each month? Write the numbers in French.)

juin _trente_   octobre _____

décembre _trente et un_   juillet _____

août _____   novembre _____

février _____   mai _____

avril						
				1	2	3
4	5	6	7	8	9	10
⑪	12	13	14	15	16	17
18	19	20	21	22	23	24
25	26	27	28	29	30	

Quelle est la date aujourd'hui? (What is today's date?)

Aujourd'hui, c'est le onze avril. (Today is the 11th of April.)

septembre						
①	2	3	4	5	6	
7	8	9	10	11	12	13
14	15	16	17	18	19	20
21	22	23	24	25	26	27
28	29	30				

Quelle est la date aujourd'hui?

Aujourd'hui, c'est le premier septembre. (Today is September 1st.)

février						
	1	2	③	4	5	6
7	8	9	10	11	12	13
14	15	16	17	18	19	20
21	22	23	24	25	26	27
28						

Écrivez les dates en français.

Quelle est la date aujourd'hui?

Aujourd'hui, c'est le trois février

décembre						
		1	2	3	4	
5	6	7	8	9	10	11
12	13	14	15	16	17	18
19	20	21	22	23	24	㉕
26	27	28	29	30	31	

Quelle est la date aujourd'hui?

_____

janvier						
				1	②	
3	4	5	6	7	8	9
10	11	12	13	14	15	16
17	18	19	20	21	22	23
24/31	25	26	27	28	29	30

Quelle est la date aujourd'hui?

_____

Quelle est la date . . .

aujourd'hui? _Aujourd'hui, c'est le quatorze octobre_

demain? (tomorrow) _le cinquante octobre_

de ton anniversaire? (your birthday) _Mon anniversaire c'est le vingtsix Avril_

de Noël? (Christmas) _____

du jour d'indépendance? (Independence Day) _____

du premier jour d'école? (the first day of school) _____

du réveillon? (New Year's Eve) _____

J'aime . . .
I like . . .

Écrivez les phrases en français.
(Write the sentences in French.)

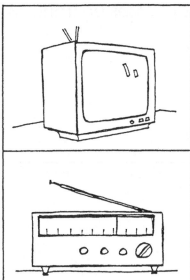

J'aime la télévision.

J'aime la télévision

J'aime la radio.

J'aime la radio

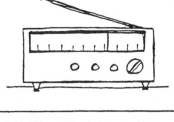

J'aime la musique.

J'aime la musique

J'aime le français.

J'aime le français

J'aime l'école.

J'aime l'école

J'aime le cinéma. J'aime le cinéma

J'aime . . .

Écrivez les phrases en français.

J'aime l'argent.

J'aime l'argent

J'aime le tennis.   *J'aime le tennis*

J'aime le football.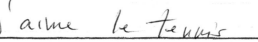

J'aime le footbll

J'aime le base-ball.

J'aime le base-ball

J'aime le raisin.

J'aime le raisin

J'aime le coca-cola.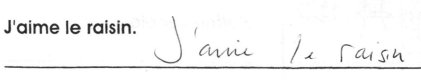

J'aime le coca-cola

J'aime beaucoup . . .
I really like . . .

Nom_____

Écrivez les phrases en français.

J'aime beaucoup le chocolat.

le chocolat

J'aime beaucoup la glace.

la glace

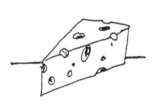

J'aime beaucoup le fromage.

le fromage

J'aime beaucoup le gâteau.

le gâteau

J'aime beaucoup les fraises.

les fraises

J'aime beaucoup les vacances.

les vacances

Je n'aime pas . . .
I don't like . . .

Nom_____

Écrivez les phrases en français.

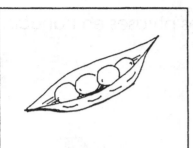

Je n'aime pas les pois.

_____

Je n'aime pas les épinards.

_____

Je n'aime pas les brocolis.

_____

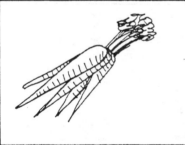

Je n'aime pas les carottes.

_____

Je n'aime pas les oignons.

_____

Je n'aime pas le raisin sec.

_____

Aimes-tu . . .?
Do you like . . .?

To ask someone you know well if he/she likes something, use the **familiar** form, **Aimes-tu . . .?**

To ask someone you do not know well or is older than you are if he/she likes something, use the **formal** form, **Aimez-vous . . .?**

Answer these questions with "**J'aime . . .**" or "**Je n'aime pas . . .**"

Exemple: (familiar)   Aimes-tu la glace? (Do you like ice cream?)

                Oui, j'aime la glace. (Yes, I like ice cream.)

       (formal)   Aimez-vous le raisin? (Do you like grapes?)

                Non, je n'aime pas le raisin. (No, I don't like grapes.)

Write a question asking each person what they think of each pictured item.

1. (your little brother)

   Aimes-tu ~~ton petit~~ frère le film?

2. (an old man)

   Aimez-vous les pois

3. (your best friend)

   Aimes-tu le coca-cola

4. (your teacher)

   Aimez-vous le français

5. (your mother)

   Aimes-tu les vacances

6. (your classmate)

   Aimes-tu les carottes

Révision

Nom_____

Write each item in the correct category in French to show whether you **like**, **like a lot**, or **dislike** each one.

J'aime . . .

_____
_____
_____
_____

J'aime beaucoup . . .

_____
_____
_____
_____

Je n'aime pas . . .

_____
_____
_____
_____

Tell whether or not you like the items pictured.

_____

_____

_____

_____

Les activités
Activities

Écrivez en français.

enseigner
(to teach)

Enseigner

danser
(to dance)

Danser

travailler
(to work)

Travailler

jouer
(to play)

Jouer

chanter
(to sing)

Chanter

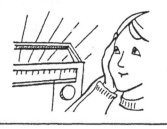

écouter la radio
(to listen to the radio)

Écouter la rado

marcher
(to walk)

Marcher

Les activités
Activities

Écrivez en français.

étudier
(to study)

Étudier

cuisiner
(to cook)

Cuisiner

nager
(to swim)

Nager

parler français
(to speak French)

Parler Français

sauter
(to jump)

Sauter

acheter
(to buy)

Acheter

regarder la télévision
(to watch television)

Les activités

Tell whether you **like**, **like a lot**, or **do not like** to do the activities in each picture.

J'aime manger

J'aime regarde le
télévisie

Je n'aime pas le travail

J'aime etudie

Je n'aime pas danse

Et toi?
And you?

Nom_____

Répondez en français. (Answer in French.)

_____

_____

_____

_____

_____

_____

_____

Les verbes en -er
-Er Verbs

Nom _____

You have learned how to speak in French about what you like and do not like to do. It is also useful to be able to tell what you and other people do.

Most verbs in French end in **-er** (chant**er** = to sing, travaill**er** = to work, nag**er** = to swim). This form of the verb is called the infinitive.

The **stem** of the verb is the infinitive minus the **-er** (example: parler–er = parl). Different endings are added to the stem for each subject.

Here are the subject pronouns and the endings for each one for the sample verb **parler**.

Parler					
Singular			**Plural**		
I	je	parl**e**	we	nous	parl**ons**
you (fam.)	tu	parl**es**			
you (formal)	vous	parl**ez**	you (pl.)	vous	parl**ez**
			they	ils/elles	parl**ent**
he/she	il/elle	parl**e**			

Study the list of verbs below.

parler	= to speak		**jouer**	= to play
chanter	= to sing		**visiter**	= to visit
nager	= to swim		**cuisiner**	= to cook
écouter	= to listen (to)		**regarder**	= to look (at)
danser	= to dance		**porter**	= to wear
étudier	= to study		**donner**	= to give

acheter = to buy   **sauter** = to jump
travailler = to work
préparer = to prepare
marcher = to walk
désirer = to want
adorer = to adore
pleurer = to cry

Les verbes en -er

Nom_____

I. Write the stems of the verbs below.

étudier _____   travailler _____   sauter _____

nager _____   donner _____   acheter _____

écouter _____   marcher _____   porter _____

chanter _____   regarder _____   téléphoner _____

II. Write the **-er** endings for each of the subject pronouns below.

tu _____   je _____   ils _____

il _____   nous_____   elles _____

vous _____   elle _____

III. Write the correct form for each subject for the verbs below.

      chanter   stem _____

je _____   il _____   vous_____

tu _____   nous_____   ils _____

      étudier   stem _____

je _____   elle _____   vous _____

tu _____   nous_____   elles _____

      porter   stem _____

je _____   il_____   vous _____

tu _____   nous_____   elles _____

Les verbes en -er

Use the pictures to write and conjugate the verbs.

verb _____   stem _____

je _____   elle _____   vous _____

tu _____   nous _____   elles _____

verb _____   stem _____

je _____   elle _____   vous _____

il _____   nous _____   elles _____

verb _____   stem _____

tu _____   elle _____   vous _____

je _____   nous _____   ils _____

verb _____   stem _____

vous _____   il _____   je _____

tu _____   nous _____   elles _____

verb _____   stem _____

tu _____   nous _____   vous _____

il _____   elle _____   je _____

verb _____   stem _____

je _____   il _____   ils _____

vous _____   nous _____   elles _____

Révision

Nom _____

I. Matching.

1. I sing.	_____	Je chante.
2. He dances.	_____	Elle écoute.
3. They talk.	_____	Nous travaillons.
4. You jump (fam.).	_____	Tu sautes.
5. She listens.	_____	Vous regardez.
6. You look (formal).	_____	Ils parlent.
7. We work.	_____	Il danse.

II. Fill in the blank with the appropriate verb form.

Elles _____   Il _____   Elle _____

Elle _____   Je _____   Vous _____

Nous _____   Tu _____   Je _____
les mathématiques.   l'espagnol.   beaucoup.

Elles _____   Ils _____   Nous _____
la télévision.   la radio.   au tennis.

Les vêtements
Clothing

Nom_____

Écrivez les mots en français.

 le manteau	le short	 le pullover	 la robe
 la jupe	 la cravate	 la chemise	 les chaussures
 les chaussettes	 les sandales	 le maillot de bain	 le blouson

Écrivez les phrases en français.

1. I like T-shirts.

_____

2. Martin is wearing shorts.

_____

3. Anne and Marie wear dresses.

_____

4. We're wearing swimming suits.

_____

5. I'm buying a tie.

6. Do you like to wear sandals?

_____

7. They're buying skirts.

_____

8. She's buying the coat.

_____

9. I like sweaters.

_____

10. He's wearing a jacket.

_____

Les questions
The Questions

Nom_____

One way to form a yes/no question in French is to reverse the order of the subject and the verb. Place a hyphen between the verb and the subject.

Exemple: Parles-tu français?

(verb) (subject)

*Remember that a question asked of **you** (addressed as tu or vous) should be answered with **I** (je). A question asked of **you** plural (vous) should be answered with **we** (nous). When the subject begins with a vowel and the verb also ends with a vowel, place a **t** between the subject and the verb.

Parle-t-il français? (Does he speak French?)
Oui, il parle français. (Yes, he speaks French.)

Parlez-vous français? (Do you (plural) speak French?)
Oui, nous parlons français. (Yes, we speak French.)

Répondez aux questions en français.
(Answer the questions in French.)

1. **Parle-t-elle français?**

   Oui, _____ .

2. **Prépare-t-elle un gâteau?**

   Oui, _____ .

3. **Écoutes-tu la radio?**

   Oui,_____ .

4. **Chantent-ils bien?**

   Non, _____ .

5. **Dansent-ils bien?**

   Oui,_____ .

6. **Études-tu l'histoire?**

   Non, _____ .

7. **Portent-elles des blousons?**

   Oui,_____ .

8. **Nagez-vous dans la piscine?**

   Oui, _____ .

Les questions

Écrivez les questions.
(Write the questions.)

1. _____?
   Non, elle ne nage pas bien.

2. _____?
   Oui, nous chantons.

3. _____?
   Non, il ne parle pas français.

4. _____?
   Oui, ils écoutent la radio.

5. _____?
   Non, je ne joue pas de la guitare.

6. _____?
   Oui, nous visitons la France.

7. _____?
   Non, elle ne porte pas de manteau.

8. _____?
   Oui, j'étudie les sciences (science).

9. _____?
   Non, ils ne dansent pas.

10. _____?
    Oui, je parle français.

11. _____?
    Non, il ne regarde pas la télévision.

12. _____?
    Oui, nous chantons.

13. _____?
    Oui, elle écoute la musique.

Salut!

Les négations
Negatives

Nom_____

To make a sentence negative, simply put the word **ne** before the verb and the word **pas** after the verb.

> **exemple:** **Je parle français.** (I speak French.)
>
> **Je ne parle pas français.** (I do **not** speak French.)

Make each sentence negative.

Ils sautent.

_____

Elles nagent.

_____

Il marche.

_____

Je regarde la télévision.

_____

Nous dansons.

_____

Elle étudie.

_____

Les questions

Nom _____

Répondez aux questions.
Answer the questions.

1. **Parles-tu anglais?**

   _____

2. **Qu'est-ce qu'il parle?**

   _____

3. **Regardent-ils la télévision?**

   _____

4. **Qu'est-ce que tu aimes?**

   _____

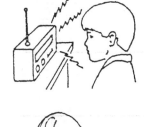

5. **Nages-tu?**

   _____

6. **Écoutez-vous la radio?**

   _____

7. **Pleure-t-elle?**

   _____

8. **Qu'est-ce que tu joues?**

   _____

9. **Chantent-elles?**

   _____

10. **Téléphonent-ils?**

    _____

11. **Qu'est-ce qu'elle étudie?**

    _____

Qu'est-ce que ça veut dire?
What does that mean?

Nom _____

Write the meanings of the questions and answers below in English.

Dansez-vous?

_____

Oui, nous dansons beaucoup.

_____

Regardes-tu la télévision?

_____

Oui, je regarde la télévision.

_____

Sautent-elles?

_____

Oui, elles sautent.

_____

Travaillent-ils?

_____

Oui, ils travaillent.

_____

Nage-t-elle?

_____

Oui, elle nage.

_____

Chantes-tu bien?

_____

Oui, je chante bien.

_____

Answering Questions Negatively

Nom_____

Respond to the following questions negatively.

exemple: **Danses-tu?** (Do you dance?)

Non, je ne danse pas. (**No**, I do **not** dance.)

Chantes-tu bien?

Non, _____

Nagent-ils?

Non, _____

Étudiez-vous?

Non, _____

Écoute-t-elle?

Non, _____

Travaillez-vous?

Non, _____

Saute-t-il bien?

Non, _____

Achète-t-il le pain?

Non, _____

Les questions
Questions

Nom_____

Answer the questions using the information in the pictures.

Écoute-t-elle la radio?

_____

Regarde-t-elle la télévision?

_____

Travaille-t-il?

_____

Danse-t-il?

_____

Chantent-ils?

_____

Nagent-ils?

_____

Parlez-vous français?

_____

Parlez-vous anglais?

_____

Regarde-t-il?

_____

Saute-t-il?

_____

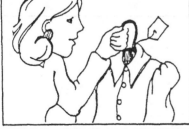

Achète-t-elle une chemise?

_____

Achète-t-elle de la glace?

_____

Qu'est-ce que c'est?
What is it?

Nom _____

Qu'est-ce que c'est?
(What is it?)

C'est une voiture.
(It's a car.)

Qu'est-ce que c'est?
(What is it?)

C'est une pomme.
(It's an apple.)

Un and **une** are **indefinite articles**. They are the equivalent of "a" or "an" in English. **Un** is used with **masculine** and **une** is used with **feminine** nouns.

Use **un** and **une** with nouns you have already learned in this book.

Qu'est-ce que c'est?

C'est _____

Qu'est-ce que c'est?

_____

Qu'est-ce que c'est?

_____

Qu'est-ce que c'est?

_____

Qu'est-ce que c'est?

_____

Qu'est-ce que c'est?

What is it?

Nom_____

If there are several things in your answer, you will need the plural of the indefinite articles. The plural of **un** is **des**. The plural of **une** is **des**. **Des** means **"some."** Sometimes we leave out the word "some" in English, but it cannot be omitted in French.

Use **des** to identify some other nouns you have learned.

Exemple:

Qu'est-ce que c'est? (What are they?)

Ce sont des fraises. (They are (some) strawberries.)

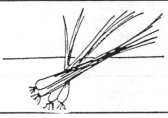

Qu'est-ce que c'est?

_____

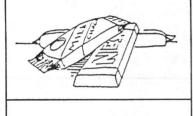

Qu'est-ce que c'est?

_____

Qu'est-ce que c'est?

_____

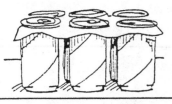

Qu'est-ce que c'est?

_____

Qu'est-ce que c'est?

_____

Qu'est-ce que c'est?

Qu'est-ce que . . . ?
What?

Nom _____

Qu'est-ce que are the words used to mean what. . . To form a question using Qu'est-ce que follow this pattern: **Qu'est-ce que** + **subject** + **verb?** The answer to this type of question will always be an object or an activity, a noun.

exemple 1: Qu'est-ce que tu achètes? (What are you buying?)

(object)   J'achète **une chemise.** (I'm buying a shirt.)

exemple 2: Qu'est-ce qu'elle fait? (What is she doing?)

(activity)   Elle **nage.** (She's swimming.)

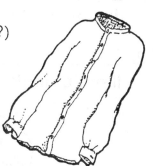

Use the pictures to answer the following questions in French.

1. **Qu'est-ce qu'il regarde?**

_____

2. **Qu'est-ce que tu étudies?**

_____

3. **Qu'est-ce qu'ils chantent?**

_____

4. **Qu'est-ce qu'elle porte?**

_____

5. **Qu'est-ce que vous jouez?**

_____

6. **Qu'est-ce que vous écoutez?**

_____

7. **Qu'est-ce que Martin achète?**

_____

8. **Qu'est-ce que tu désires?**

_____

9. **Qu'est-ce qu'il parle?**

_____

10. **Qu'est-ce que Marie prépare?**

_____

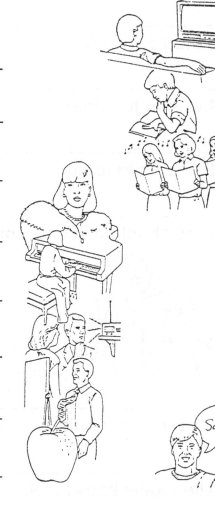

41

Les questions

Nom_____

1. <u>Qu'est-ce que tu aimes?</u>
   J'aime la glace.

2. _____?
   Il parle anglais.

3. _____?
   Je porte un pantalon.

4. _____?
   Nous jouons du piano.

5. _____?
   J'étudie l'histoire.

6. _____?
   Nous visitons la France.

7. _____?
   Il écoute la radio.

8. _____?
   Elles chantent la chanson.

9. _____?
   Je regarde la télévision.

10. _____?
    Elles répondent aux questions.

11. _____?
    J'aime le français.

12. _____?
    Elle étudie l'espagnol.

13. _____?
    Nous achetons le pain.

Le français

Les adjectifs
Adjectives

Nom_____

An **adjective** is a word that describes a noun. In French **all nouns have gender**. They are either masculine or feminine. Each adjective **must agree** with the **gender** of the noun it describes. So adjectives in French have both masculine and feminine forms. Use the form that agrees with the gender of the noun.

Singular feminine adjectives often end in **-e.** Singular masculine ones often do not. Since singular feminine adjectives end in **-e,** the final consonant is pronounced. It is not pronounced in singular masculine adjectives.

The adjectives below are masculine. Make them feminine.

1. **français** (French) _____

2. **excellent** (excellent) _____

3. **brun** (dark-haired) _____

4. **blond** (blond) _____

5. **intelligent** (intelligent) _____

6. **laid** (ugly) _____

7. **petit** (small) _____

8. **intéressant** (interesting) _____

9. **grand** (tall) _____

Les adjectifs

Nom _____

Adjectives in French must agree in **number** as well as **gender**. That is, if the noun is singular, then the adjective describing it must also be singular. If the noun is plural, then the adjective must also be plural.

To make an adjective plural . . .

1. add **-s**

exemple: grand   **>**   grands

Most adjectives have four forms:

	singular	plural
masculine	grand	grands
feminine	grande	grandes

If a group contains both masculine and feminine nouns, use the masculine plural form.

> **exemple:** Les garçons et les filles sont grand**s**.
> (The boys and the girls are tall.)

Fill in the blanks with the correct form of the underlined adjective in each phrase. **Remember:** Some adjectives change form because of gender.

1. <u>small</u> girls = **les** _____ **filles**

2. <u>interesting</u> books = **les livres** _____

3. <u>blond</u> men = **les hommes** _____

4. <u>intelligent</u> people = **les gens** _____

5. <u>French</u> tests = **les examens** _____

6. <u>interesting</u> classes = **les classes** _____

7. <u>pretty</u> women = **les** _____ **femmes**

8. <u>intelligent</u> teachers = **les professeurs** _____

9. <u>ugly</u> houses = **les maisons** _____

10. <u>big</u> trees = **les** _____ **arbres**

11. <u>French</u> boys = **les garçons** _____

12. <u>excellent</u> fathers = **les pères** _____

Les adjectifs

Nom_____

There are many adjectives that end in **-e.** These keep the same spelling no matter with which type of singular noun, masculine or feminine, they are used.

exemple: une fille **modeste**   un garçon **modeste**

Several adjectives of this type are . . .

modeste = modest   **pauvre** = poor   **sévère** = strict

célèbre = famous   **stupide** = stupid   **difficile** = hard

bête = dumb/stupid   **riche** = rich   **triste** = sad

irrésistible = irresistible   **facile** = easy   **timide** = shy

formidable = great   **jeune** = young   **sympathique** = nice

optimiste = optimistic   **pessimiste** = pessimistic

Write the correct forms of the adjectives below.

1. an irresistible boy = **un garçon** _____

2. a great car = **une voiture** _____

3. a famous woman = **une femme** _____

4. a nice man = **un homme** _____

5. a stupid animal = **un animal** _____

6. a sad girl = **une fille** _____

7. an easy test = **un examen** _____

8. a rich man = **un homme** _____

9. an optimistic woman = **une femme** _____

10. a young student = **un étudiant** _____

11. a great book = **un livre** _____

12. a shy boy = **un garçon** _____

13. a strict father = **un père** _____

14. an easy question = **une question** _____

15. a hard test = **un examen** _____

16. a sad brother = **un frère** _____

Les adjectifs

Nom _____

Écrivez la bonne forme des adjectifs.

1. (big) **une** _____ maison

2. (short) **un** _____ homme

3. (blond) **une fille** _____

4. (dark-haired) **les hommes** _____

5. (small) **une** _____ classe

6. (excellent) **un livre** _____

7. (pretty) **les** _____ filles

8. (funny) **le professeur** _____

9. (small) **une** _____ maison

10. (mean) **le chien** _____

11. (ugly) **un monstre** _____

12. (tall) **un** _____ éléphant

13. (thin) **un garçon** _____

14. (nice) **un homme** _____

15. (perfect) **un jour** _____

16. (elegant) **une femme** _____

17. (intelligent) **une fille** _____

18. (content) **un garçon** _____

19. (patient) **une tortue** _____

20. (smart) **un lapin** _____

21. (big) **un** _____ animal

22. (nice) **un professeur** _____

23. (tall) **les** _____ filles

24. (blond) **un homme** _____

Être
To be

The verb **être** (to be) is used with adjectives to describe people or things. The verb **être** does not follow a regular pattern like the -**er** verbs. It is an irregular verb.

Être			
je	**suis**	nous	**sommes**
tu	**es**	vous	**êtes**
il	**est**	ils	**sont**
elle	**est**	elles	**sont**

Conjugate the verb **être** with the adjective **grand**. (The adjective must also agree with the subject.

1. Je (masc.) _____ _____
2. Tu _____ _____
3. Vous (sing.) _____ _____
4. Il _____ _____
5. Elle _____ _____

6. Nous _____ _____
7. Je (fem.) _____ _____
8. Vous (pl.) _____ _____
9. Ils _____ _____
10. Elles _____ _____

Conjugate the verb **être** with the following adjectives.

petit (short)

1. Je (masc.) _____ _____
2. Tu (masc.) _____ _____
3. Elle _____ _____

4. Nous _____ _____
5. Ils _____ _____
6. Vous (sing.) _____ _____

intelligent (intelligent)

1. Tu _____ _____
2. Elles _____ _____
3. Nous_____ _____
4. Je (fem.) _____ _____

5. Vous (sing.) _____ _____
6. Il _____ _____
7. Ils_____ _____
8. Vous (pl.) _____ _____

Être

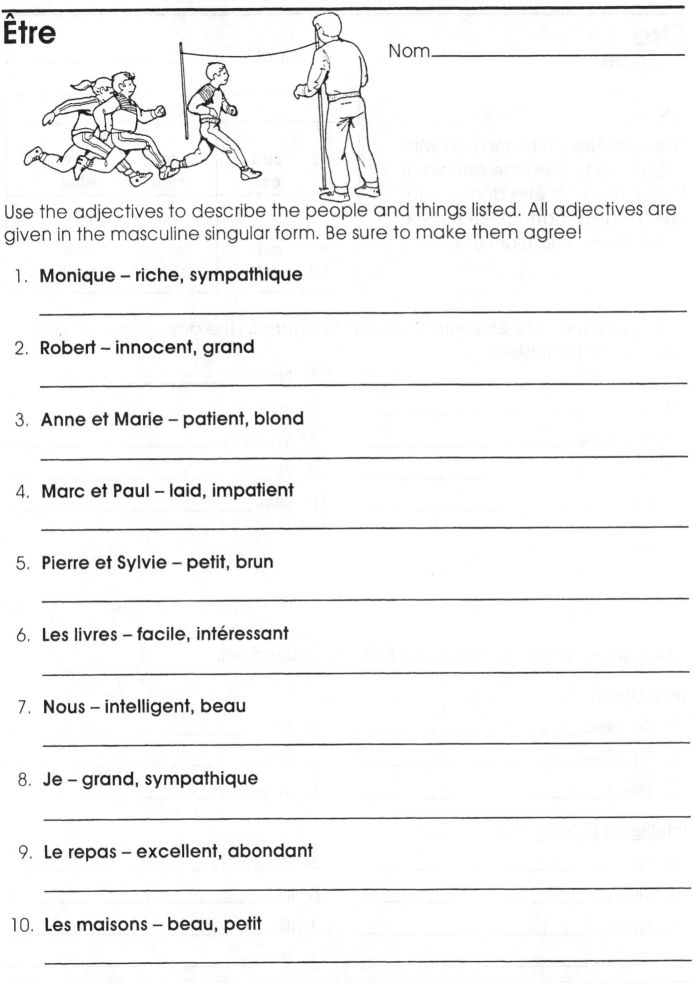

Nom_____

Use the adjectives to describe the people and things listed. All adjectives are given in the masculine singular form. Be sure to make them agree!

1. **Monique – riche, sympathique**

_____

2. **Robert – innocent, grand**

_____

3. **Anne et Marie – patient, blond**

_____

4. **Marc et Paul – laid, impatient**

_____

5. **Pierre et Sylvie – petit, brun**

_____

6. **Les livres – facile, intéressant**

_____

7. **Nous – intelligent, beau**

_____

8. **Je – grand, sympathique**

_____

9. **Le repas – excellent, abondant**

_____

10. **Les maisons – beau, petit**

_____

Les questions avec le verbe être

Nom _____

Répondez aux questions. (Answer the questions.)
Use the pictures as clues for your answers.

exemple: Est-ce que Michel est riche?

Oui, il est riche.

Est-ce que François est bête?

Non, il n'est pas bête.

(intelligent) Il est intelligent.

1. **La maîtresse est-elle sévère?**

_____

2. **Es-tu petit?**

_____

(grand) _____

3. **Est-ce que les singes sont drôles?**

_____

4. **Êtes-vous patientes?**

_____

5. **Est-ce que Laurence est brune?**

_____

(blond) _____

6. **Le livre est-il intéressant?**

_____

(ennuyeux) _____

7. **Est-ce qu'Albert est gros?**

_____

8. **Est-ce que Jeanne est sympathique?**

_____

(méchant) _____

Les professions
Professions

Nom_____

Some common professions are . . .

		un musicien	= a musician
une infirmière	= a nurse	**un dentiste**	= a dentist
une secrétaire	= a secretary	**un journaliste**	= a journalist
un ingénieur	= an engineer	**un directeur**	= a manager
un avocat	= a lawyer	**un agriculteur**	= a farmer
un mécanicien	= a mechanic	**un ouvrier**	= a factory worker
un tecnicien	= a technician	**un écrivain**	= a writer
un pilote	= a pilot	**un poète**	= a poet
un cuisinier	= a cook	**un danseur**	= a dancer (masc.)
un photographe	= a photographer	**une danseuse**	= a dancer (fem.)

Les professions

Nom _____

Indefinite articles (un, une) are not used with the professions after the verb **être** unless they are modified by an adjective.

exemples: Colette est chanteuse. (Colette is a singer.)

Colette est **une** bonne chanteuse. (Colette is a good singer.)

Fill in the blanks with the correct form of **être** and the indicated professions.

1. Je _____ .
(artist)

2. Emmanuel _____ .
(mechanic)

3. Nous _____ .
(journalist)

4. Anita _____ .
(nurse)

5. Monsieur Dulac _____ .
(musician)

6. Whitney Houston _____ .
(singer)

7. Mark Twain _____ .
(writer)

8. Ma mère _____ .
(secretary)

9. Mon père _____ .
(pilot)

10. Vous _____ .
(cook)

11. Patricia _____ .
(dentist)

12. Tu _____ .
(photographer)

13. Elles _____ .
(lawyer)

14. Jean_____ .
(dancer)

15. Elle _____ .
(teacher)

L'heure
The Time

To answer **Quelle heure est-il?** (What is the time?) follow the patterns below. Write the times as indicated.

Il est une heure.

_____

Il est deux heures.

_____

Il est minuit.

_____

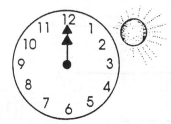

Il est midi.

_____

Il est cinq heures cinq.

_____

Il est huit heures un quart.

_____

L'heure

Écrivez l'heure de chaque réveil. (Write the times shown on the clocks.)

Il est onze heure vingt-cinq.

_____

Il est neuf heures et demie.

_____

Il est dix heures moins vingt.

_____

Il est dix heures moins le quart.

_____

Il est dix heures moins dix.

_____

Il est dix heures moins cinq.

_____

L'heure

Écrivez les heures de chaque réveil.

_____

_____

_____

_____

_____

_____

L'heure

Nom _____

À is used to tell **at** what time something will take place.

exemple: À quelle heure est le cours d'espagnol? (**At** what time is the Spanish class?)

   Le cours est à huit heures. (The class is **at** eight o'clock.)

To be more specific about the time use . . .

du matin   = in the morning/a.m.

de l'après-midi = in the afternoon/p.m.

du soir   = in the evening/p.m.

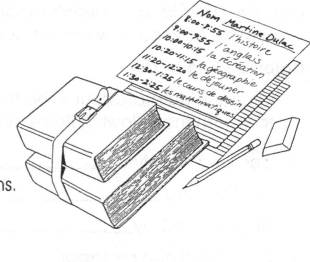

Regardez l'horaire et répondez aux questions.
(Look at the schedule
and answer the questions.)
Be sure to include a.m. or p.m.

1. **À quelle heure est le cours d'anglais?**

_____

2. **À quelle heure est le déjeuner?**

_____

3. **À quelle heure est le cours de géographie?**

_____

4. **À quelle heure est le cours de dessin?**

_____

5. **À quelle heure est la récréation?**

_____

6. **À quelle heure est le cours de mathématiques?**

_____

7. **À quelle heure est le cours d'histoire?**

_____

8. **À quelle heure finissent les cours?**

_____

Les adjectifs possessifs
Possessive Adjectives

One way to indicate possession is to use a noun followed by **de** and the owner's name. Use the masculine form **(du)** or the feminine form **(de la)** with nouns. (There are **no** apostrophes in French.)

la maison **de** Pierre = Pierre's house

  le livre **de** Martine = Martine's book

Note: de + le = du

    la chaise **du** professeur = the teacher's chair

Tell to whom the following items belong.

1. bedroom/Martine _____

2. books/Pierre _____

3. bicycle/the boy_____

4. apartment/the professor _____

5. pencil/the girl _____

6. dog/the Proust family_____

Another way to indicate possession is to use possessive adjectives: my, your, his, her, etc.

	Singular		Plural
	Masculine	Feminine	
my	**mon**	**ma**	**mes**
your (fam.)	**ton**	**ta**	**tes**
your (form. and pl.)	**votre**	**votre**	**vos**
his, her	**son**	**sa**	**ses**
their	**leur**	**leur**	**leurs**
our	**notre**	**notre**	**nos**

Like other adjectives, a possessive adjective must agree in gender and number with the noun it modifies. (Note that the adjective agrees with the **noun** it modifies, not with the **owner**.)

exemples: mon livre = my book

            mes livres = my books

        notre chien = our dog

    notre maison = our house

        nos frères = our brothers

         nos soeurs = our sisters

Révision

Nom_____

Tell that the following items belong to you.

  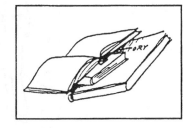

_____   _____   _____

_____   _____   _____

Tell that the following items belong to your brother.

 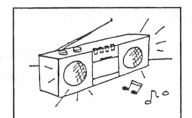 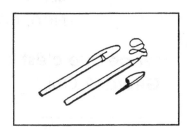

_____   _____   _____

_____   _____   _____

Tell that the following items belong to both of you.

_____   _____   _____

_____   _____   _____

Tell that the following items belong to your friends.

  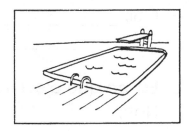

_____   _____   _____

_____   _____   _____

La curiosité
Curiosity

You and a new friend are walking to school. Your friend asks you questions about everything he sees. Answer his questions as indicated.

exemples: Est-ce que c'est la maison d'Emmanuel?
Oui, c'est sa maison.

Est-ce que c'est la maison de Suzanne?
Non, ce n'est pas sa maison.

1. **Est-ce que c'est la soeur de George?** Oui, _____
_____

2. **Est-ce que c'est le chat de Monsieur Dulac?** Non, _____
_____

3. **Est-ce que ce sont les frères d'Anita?** Oui, _____
_____

4. **Est-ce que ce sont les parents de Philippe?** Non, _____
_____

5. **Est-ce que c'est votre voiture?**
Oui, _____
_____

6. **Est-ce que c'est notre autobus?**
Non, _____
_____

7. **Est-ce que ce sont les livres de Jean et de Michel?** Oui, _____
_____

8. **Est-ce que c'est la classe de Madame Joly?** Non, _____
_____

9. **Est-ce que ce sont les chaises des filles?** Oui, _____
_____

10. **Est-ce que c'est mon lycée?** Non,
_____
_____

11. **Est-ce que c'est l'école de ton frère?** Oui, _____
_____

12. **Est-ce que ce sont les professeurs de notre lycée?** Non, _____
_____

Allons à . . .
Let's go to . . .

Nom_____

To indicate location use the prepositions **à, en,** or **au** meaning "at" or "to." **À** goes with feminine words, **en** goes with feminine countries, and **au** goes with masculine countries and words.

exemples: Elle va **en** Californie. (She's going to California.—**la** Californie)
Je vais **à** la montagne. (I'm going to the mountains.)
Je vais **au** marché. (I'm going to the market—**le** marché)

 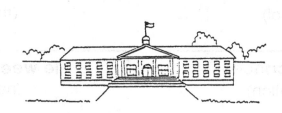 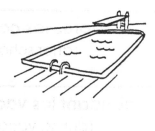

Écrivez où vont les gens.

1. **Anita va** _____
(swimming pool)

2. **Marc va** _____
(café)

3. **Nous allons**_____
(house)

4. **Les enfants vont**_____
(concert)

5. **Je vais**_____
(library)

6. **Elles vont** _____
(movie theatre)

7. **Tu vas** _____
(country)

8. **Vous allez**_____
(bank)

Quand?
When?

Nom_____

Écrivez les expressions.

aujourd'hui
(today)

cet après-midi
(this afternoon)

demain
(tomorrow)

ce soir
(tonight)

après les cours
(after school)

ce week-end
(this weekend)

pendant les vacances
(during vacation)

le week-end prochain
(next weekend)

ce matin
(this morning)

la semaine prochaine
(next week)

Write in French when you will do the following activities as indicated.

1. **mes devoirs** (my homework)

_____ (this afternoon)

2. **aller au lit** (go to bed)

_____ (tonight)

3. **se relaxer** (relax)

_____ (during vacation)

4. **aller nager** (go swimming)

_____ (next week)

5. **faire du vélo** (ride my bike)

_____ (after school)

6. **jouer au ballon** (play ball)

_____ (tomorrow)

7. **visiter ma grand-mère** (visit my grandma)

_____ (this weekend)

8. **manger le petit déjeuner** (eat breakfast)

_____ (this morning)

9. **aller au cinéma** (go to a movie)

_____ (today)

10. **aller en voyage** (take a trip)

_____ (next weekend)

Comment?
How?

Nom _____

Comment, when used with a subject pronoun (je, tu, il, elle, nous, vous, ils, elles), can be used to describe someone.

exemples: **Comment** sont-elles?

Elles sont tristes.

Comment est-il?

Il est riche.

Repondez aux questions.

1. **Comment es-tu?** (timid) _____

   _____

2. **Comment êtes-vous?** (young) _____

   _____

3. **Comment sont-elles?** (pessimistic) _____

   _____

4. **Comment est-il?** (blond) _____

   _____

5. **Comment sont-ils?** (polite) _____

   _____

6. **Comment est-elle?** (nice) _____

   _____

7. **Comment es-tu?** (little) _____

   _____

8. **Comment est-elle?** (famous) _____

   _____

9. **Comment êtes-vous?** (modest) _____

   _____

10. **Comment sont-ils?** (stupid) _____

    _____

11. **Comment sont-elles?** (intelligent) _____

    _____

12. **Comment est-il?** (sad) _____

    _____

Où?
Where?

The phrases below can be used to answer the question "**Où?**" Écrivez en français.

à la campagne

_____

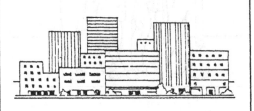

en ville

_____

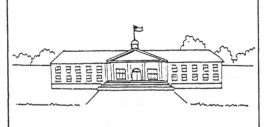

au lycée

_____

au restaurant

_____

à la plage

_____

à l'aéroport

_____

Où?

Écrivez les phrases en français.

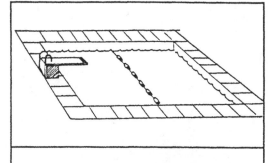

à la piscine

_____

à la maison

_____

au cinéma

_____

au bureau

_____

au théatre

_____

aux États-Unis

_____

Où est-ce?
Where is it?

Nom_____

exemple: C'est près de Marie. (It's near Marie.)

Écrivez en français.

près de (near)

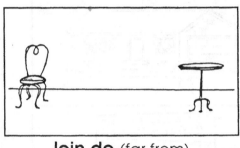

loin de (far from)

sur (on top of)

sous (under)

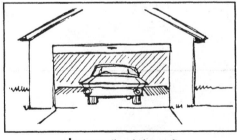

dans (inside of)

à l'extérieur de (outside of)

Où est-ce?

Nom _____

à la droite de (to the right of)

à la gauche de (to the left of)

en face de (in front of)

derrière (behind/in back of)

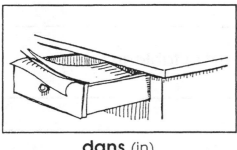

dans (in)

au-dessus (above)

à côté de (beside/next to)

entre (between)

Où est-ce?

Répondez en français. (Give one answer for each line.)

1. **Où sont les livres?**

_____

5. **Où est le drapeau** (flag)**?**

_____

2. **Où est le professeur?**

_____

6. **Où est le tableau?**

_____

_____

3. **Où est Anne?**

_____

_____

7. **Où est André?**

_____

_____

_____

4. **Où est Pierre?**

_____

_____

8. **Où est la pomme?**

_____

_____

Où?

Answer the questions according to the pictures.

Où est Cécile?

_____

Où est Jean?

_____

Où es-tu?

_____

Où sont-ils?

_____

Où êtes-vous?

_____

Où êtes-vous?

_____

Où?

Answer the questions according to the pictures.

Où nagent Georges et Françoise?

_____

Où travaille Martine?

_____

Où sont les gens?

_____

Où étudies-tu?

_____

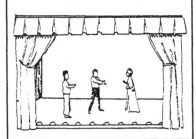

Où sont les acteurs?

_____

Où est l'avion?

_____

Où s'achète . . . ?
Where does one buy . . . ?

Nom_____

Écrivez en français. **Où s'achète . . .**

le pain?

à la boulangerie

les gâteaux?

à la pâtisserie

la viande?

à la boucherie

les glaces?

chez le glacier

les fruits?

chez le fruitier

le poisson?

à la poissonnerie

les médicaments?

à la pharmacie

l'alimentation?

au supermarché

Où s'achète . . . ?

Nom_____

Répondez en français.

1. **Qu'achètes-tu chez le glacier?**
   <u>J'achète des glaces.</u>

2. **Qu'achètes-tu à la boulangerie?**
   _____

3. **Qu'achètes-tu à la boucherie?**
   _____

4. **Qu'achètes-tu à la pâtisserie?**
   _____

5. **Qu'achètes-tu à la poissonnerie?**
   _____

6. **Qu'achètes-tu au supermarché?**
   _____

7. **Qu'achètes-tu chez le fruitier?**
   _____

Vocabulaire

Vocabulary

Nom_____

```
P W S A A E H T T L U D R T H O E X
A L A M U S I Q U E E A I H A L T C
R A L R P R L S D L A F U A O N W S
L L E L N O E E K E O R C E I E T
E A C L E L R G S T E F E O E E S
R P I I A S E T A F U L R I M E S T
I A N S A B U D E E R D C U D A U V
A T E L H T O P R R E A I A I N G S
O I M A G A A U E A M M I E I T C E
S S A B R N T R L R P E D S R N R A
S S I O U A E N A A M E I T E A R T
H E O U T T N H T S N A A U E S N A
E R Y C E A P O I S R G R U M E E H
E I X H A A U E E E F I E C G D O X
B E C E L E N I L O E E E R H E O E
K A T R A V A I L L E R A B I E W T
T T B I S F T W S T E L A T A E R N
A E T E H E L T C H A N T E R T D I
```

Traduissez les mots et trouvez les mots en français.
(Translate the words and find the French translations.)

flag	money
bakery	strawberries
butcher shop	grapes
pastry shop	to sing
supermarket	to buy
fruit	to speak
pharmacy	to study
music	to work
school	to wear
movie theater	cheese

Aller
To go

Nom_____

Aller (to go) is an irregular verb.

Aller is usually followed by **à** (to).

Some places you might go are . . .

Aller			
je	**vais**	nous	**allons**
tu	**vas**	vous	**allez**
il	**va**	ils	**vont**
elle	**va**	elles	**vont**

la bibliotèque = the library

le café = the café

le musée = the museum

le lycée = the school

le parc = the park

l'hotel = the hotel

la gare = the train station

Answer the following questions using **aller à** and the place in the picture.

1. **Où vas-tu?**

_____

2. **Où va Laurence?**

_____

3. **Où vont Jean et Christophe?**

_____

4. **Où allez-vous?**

_____

5. **Où vont les touristes?**

_____

6. **Où allez-vous?**

_____

7. **Où va Jean-Luc?**

_____

8. **Où va Pascale?**

_____

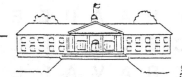

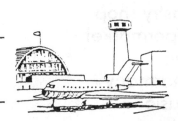

Aller

Aller is followed by **an infinitive** to tell what is going to happen in the future.

> **exemple:** Je **vais voyager** demain. (I'm going to travel tomorrow.)

Tell what the following people are going to do tomorrow by combining the given elements.

> **exemple: Pierre/travailler**
> <u>Pierre va travailler demain.</u>

1. **Cécile/chanter** _____

2. **Christine et Anne/danser** _____

3. **Les enfants/étudier** _____

4. **Je/marcher** _____

5. **Nous/répondre** _____

6. **Les soeurs/visiter** _____

7. **Emmanuel/travailler** _____

If you make a sentence with two verbs negative, be sure to put **ne** before the first verb and **pas** after the first verb..

> **exemple:** Non, je **ne** vais **pas** chanter. (No, I'm not going to sing.)

Répondez aux questions en français.

1. **Vas-tu étudier demain?** Oui, _____

2. **Allez-vous manger ce soir?** Oui, _____

3. **Aller-vous parler en classe?** Non, _____

4. **Va-t-elle écouter?** Oui, _____

5. **Va-t-il regarder la télévision?** Non, _____

6. **Allez-vous acheter des vêtements?** Non, _____

7. **Vas-tu nager demain?** Oui, _____

L'impératif
The Imperative

When you tell someone to do something you use the command form of a verb, the **imperative** (l'impératif).

To give a command to someone you know well using a regular verb, use the **tu** form of the verb minus the -**s**. As in English, the "you" (tu) is understood.

exemple: Tu danses. (You dance/are dancing.)

        Danse!   (Dance!)

Tell your friend to do the following things:

Sing! _____

Speak French! _____

Watch TV! _____

Swim! _____

Eat! _____

Listen! _____

Study! _____

Cook! _____

To give a command to someone you address in a formal way, use the formal form without the pronoun.

exemple: Vous dansez.   (You dance/are dancing.)

        Dansez!   (Dance!)

To practice, tell your older neighbor to do the following things:

Sing! _____   Eat! _____

Speak French! _____   Listen! _____

Watch TV! _____   Study! _____

Swim! _____   Cook! _____

L'impératif

The command form for **nous** (Let's dance!, Let's sing!) is the same as the conjugated form of the verb for **nous.** The subject pronoun (nous) is omitted since it is understood.

exemples: **Dansons!**   Let's dance!
Chantons!   Let's sing!
Parlons!   Lets talk!

Écrivez l'impératif. Write the imperative form of the verb.

1. **Eat!** (vous) _____

2. **Jump!** (vous) _____

3. **Sing!** (tu) _____

4. **Let's dance!** _____

5. **Dance!** (vous) _____

6. **Let's work!** _____

7. **Look!** (tu) _____

8. **Sing!** (vous) _____

9. **Let's look!** _____

10. **Jump!** (tu) _____

11. **Dance!** (tu) _____

12. **Listen!** (vous) _____

13. **Work!** (vous) _____

14. **Look!** (vous) _____

Avoir
To have

Nom _____

Avoir (to have) is an important irregular verb.

Avoir is usually followed by a noun.

    exemple: J'**ai** une radio.

Avoir			
j' (je)	**ai**	nous	**avons**
tu	**as**	vous	**avez**
il	**a**	ils	**ont**
elle	**a**	elles	**ont**

Using the pictures, tell what the following people have.

la guitare

1. **Marc** _____

les disques

2. **Je** _____

la maison

3. **Anne** _____

les livres

4. **Nous** _____

le crayon

5. **Elle** _____

le popcorn

6. _____ **vous** (sing.)**?**

les chiens

7. **Ils** _____

le papier

8. _____ **vous** (pl.)**?**

la bicyclette

9. **Tu** _____

la pomme

10. **Nous** _____

les chaussures

11. **Elles** _____

la voiture

12. **Monsieur Dulac** _____

À la maison
At home

Écrivez les mots en français.

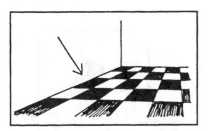

le sol

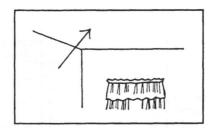

le plafond

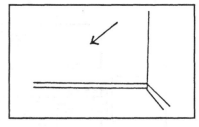

le mur

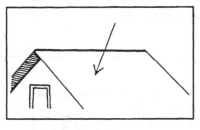

le toit

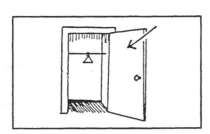

la porte

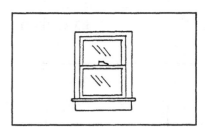

la fenêtre

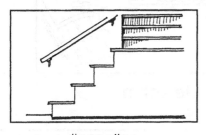

l'escalier

la cheminée

le tapis

les rideaux

le placard

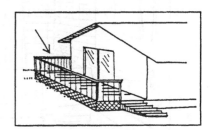

la terrasse

À la maison

Nom _____

Écrivez les mots en français.

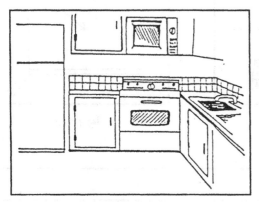

la cuisine

la chambre

la salle à manger

le salon

la salle de bain

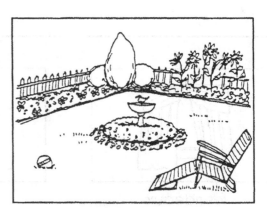

le jardin

La famille Dulac

Nom _____

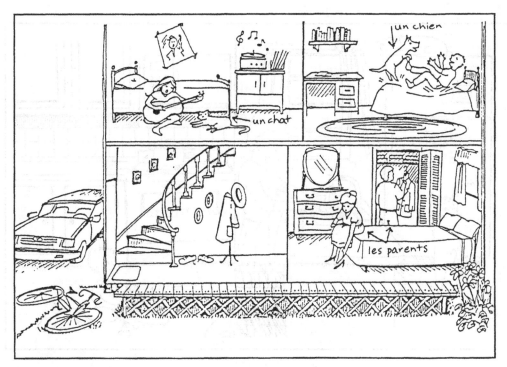

Répondez aux questions.

1. **Est-ce que la famille Dulac a une grande maison?**

   _____

2. **Quels animaux ont-ils?**

   _____

3. **Est-ce que la maison a une cuisine?**

   _____

4. **Combien de pièces y a-t-il dans la maison?**

   _____

5. **Est-ce qu'il y a un jardin?**

   _____

6. **Est-ce que la maison a une terrasse?**

   _____

7. **Qu'y a-t-il dans la chambre des parents?**

   _____

8. **Est-ce que la maison a une cheminée?**

   _____

9. **Y a-t-il un tapis dans le salon?**

   _____

10. **La maison a-t-elle un escalier?**

   _____

11. **Y a-t-il des rideaux aux fenêtres?**

   _____

12. **Où est le chat?**

   _____

La cuisine

Répondez aux questions.

1. **Est-ce qu'il y a un lave-vaisselle?**

   _____

2. **Est-ce qu'il y a un chat?**

   _____

3. **Est-ce qu'il y a un enfant?**

   _____

4. **Est-ce qu'il y a un four à micro-ondes?**

   _____

5. **Est-ce qu'il y a une cuisinière?**

   _____

6. **Est-ce qu'il y a un frigidaire?**

   _____

7. **Est-ce qu'il y a un évier?**

   _____

8. **Est-ce qu'il y a des assiettes?**

   _____

9. **Est-ce qu'il y a un jouet?**

   _____

10. **Est-ce qu'il y a une femme?**

   _____

L'âge
Age

Nom_____

The verb **avoir** is used to talk about age.

Quel âge as-tu? (How old are you?)

J'ai quatorze ans. (I'm 14 years old.)

Ask how old the subjects are in parentheses and respond using the numbers indicated. Use the pattern: **subject + avoir + number + ans**

exemple: **(elle)** <u>Quel âge a-t-elle?</u>

(30) <u>Elle a trente ans.</u>

1. **(tu)** _____

   (15) _____

2. **(vous)** _____

   (10) _____

3. **(il)** _____

   (21) _____

4. **(vous)** _____

   (80) _____

5. **(Monique)** _____

   (13) _____

6. **(l'enfant)** _____

   (1) _____

7. **(tu)** _____

   (4) _____

8. **(elles)** _____

   (18) _____

9. **(Madame Dulac)** _____

   (95) _____

10. **(Françoise et David)** _____

    (40) _____

La faim et la soif
Hunger and Thirst

Nom_____

The verb **avoir** is also used when you are talking about **hunger** and **thirst**.

avoir faim = to be hungry
J'ai faim. = I am hungry.

avoir soif = to be thirsty
Il a soif. = He is thirsty.

State that the following people are hungry or thirsty as indicated.

1. **Nous/faim**

   _____

2. **Elles/soif**

   _____

3. **Tu/faim**

   _____

4. **Elle/soif**

   _____

5. **Vous/faim**

   _____

Répondez aux questions.

1. **Est-ce que Georges a soif?**

   Oui, _____

2. **As-tu faim?**

   Oui, _____

3. **Est-ce que Monsieur Dulac a très faim?**

   Oui, _____

4. **Avez-vous très soif?**

   Non, _____

5. **Est-ce que Colette a soif?**

   Non, _____

6. **Avez-vous très soif?**

   Oui, _____

7. **Est-ce que les enfants ont faim?**

   Non, _____

Le chaud et le froid
Hot and Cold

Nom_____

Another set of expressions using **avoir** are:

avoir chaud = to be hot/to feel hot   **avoir froid** = to be cold/to feel cold

Tell how the following people would feel according to the temperature.

1. **je/90°F**

_____

2. **elle/10°F**

_____

3. **nous/40°F**

_____

4. **tu/86°F**

_____

5. **vous/0°F**

_____

Tell how the following people feel based on how they are dressed.

1. **Emmanuel porte un manteau.**

_____

2. **Madame Dulac est en maillot de bain.**

_____

3. **Je porte un pullover et un pantalon.**

_____

4. **Vous portez un short et une chemise.**

_____

Note: In France the Celsius temperature is used.

Can you tell how these people feel using the centigrade thermometer?

1. **Elles/5°C**

_____

2. **Il/30°C**

_____

Faire
To do

Faire is an important ir-regular verb. It is used in many expressions.

It means **to do** or **to make**.

Faire			
je	**fais**	nous	**faisons**
tu	**fais**	vous	**faites**
il	**fait**	ils	**font**
elle	**fait**	elles	**font**

exemple:

Que **fais**-tu? (What are you doing./What do you do?)
Je **fais** mes devoirs. (I'm doing homework./I do homework.)

Expressions using **faire**.

faire ses devoirs = to do homework   **faire la fête** = to have a party
faire des projets = to make plans   **faire un barbecue** = to have a barbeque
faire un picnic = to have a picnic   **faire sa valise** = to pack your suitcase

Que font-ils?

Ils _____   Elle _____   Emmanuel _____

Vous _____   Je _____   Tu _____

_____

Le temps
The Weather

Faire is also used in some expressions to talk about the weather.

Quel temps fait-il? (What's the weather like?)

Écrivez en français.

Il fait beau.
(The weather's nice.)

Il fait mauvais.
(The weather's bad.)

Il fait froid.
(It's cold out.)

Il fait chaud.
(It's hot out.)

Il fait du soleil.
(It's sunny.)

Il fait du vent.
(It's windy.)

These expressions do **not** use faire.

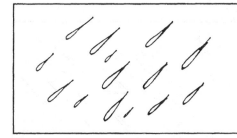

Il pleut.
(It's raining.)

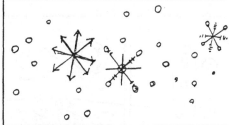

Il neige.
(It's snowing.)

Il y a des nuages.
(It's cloudy.)

Quel temps fait-il sur les photos?

Nom_____

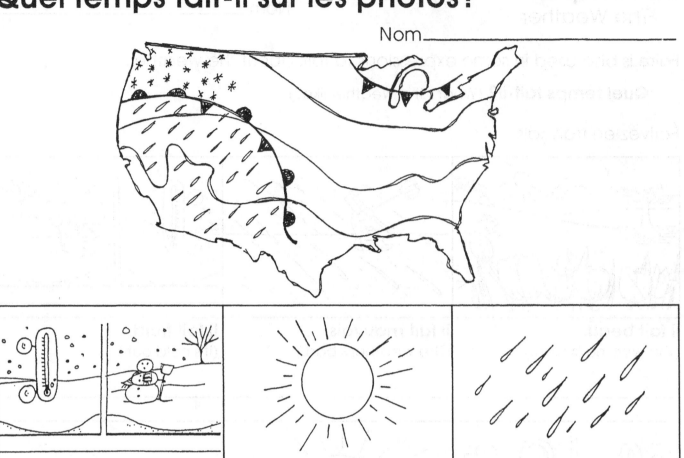

Les saisons
The Seasons

Nom _____

le printemps

l'été

l'automne

l'hiver

Quel temps fait-il au printemps?

1._____

2._____

3._____

Quel temps fait-il en été?

1._____

2._____

3._____

Quel temps fait-il en hiver?

1._____

2._____

3._____

Quel temps fait-il en automne?

1._____

2._____

3._____

Les sports
Sports

Jouer is a verb used to talk about sports. It means to play.

   exemples: Elle **joue** au volley-ball.

            Ils **jouent** au football.

Écrivez en français.

au football

au volley-ball

au base-ball

au tennis

le basket-ball

au football américain

Tell which sport the following people are playing.

Il_____ **Elles**_____ **Nous**_____ **Je**_____

_____   _____   _____   _____

Pour pratiquer les sports
To Practice Sports

Nom _____

Here are some objects we use to play various sports. Écrivez en français.

une raquette

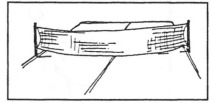

un filet

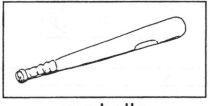

une balle

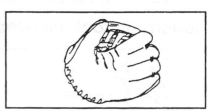

un gant

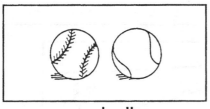

une batte

un ballon

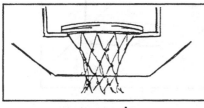

un panier

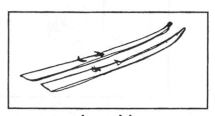

des skis

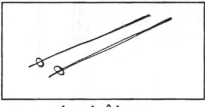

des bâtons

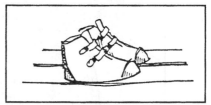

des chaussures de ski

Pour pratiquer les sports

Tell which items are necessary to participate in each sport shown.

1. Nous jouons au football avec _____

2. Nous jouons au base-ball avec _____

3. Nous jouons au basket-ball avec _____

4. Nous jouons au tennis avec _____

Les comparaisons
Comparisons

To compare two things or people in French use the following:

plus + adjective + que.

(more _____ than)

exemple: Antoine est plus grand que Paul.

(Antoine is taller than Paul.)

Note: Remember that adjectives must agree in gender and number with the nouns they modify.

exemples: Anne est plus grande que Marie.

Les voitures sont plus grandes que les bicyclettes.

Write statements in French comparing the following people and things using the adjectives given.

Michel 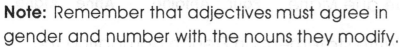 **Albert**

1. **(gros)** _____

_____

Mimi **Bruno**

2. **(beau)** _____

_____

Claudine

Hélène

3. **(brun)** _____

_____

la fraise

la pomme

4. **(grand)** _____

_____

l'éléphant

le chat

5. **(petit)** _____

_____

Les comparaisons

Nom _____

Another way to compare two people or things is to use:

moins + adjective + que.

(less _____ than)

exemples: Paul est **moins** grand **qu'**Antoine.

(Paul is less tall than Antoine.)

Anne est moins grand**e** que Marie.

Paul   **Antoine**   **Anne**   **Marie**

Write statements in French comparing the
following people and things using **moins**/**que**.

la voiture

la bicyclette

1. **(grand)** _____

_____

Paul   Robert

2. **(sympathique)** _____

_____

la télévision   le film

3. **(intéressant)** _____

_____

Estèle

Catherine

4. **(intelligent)** _____

_____

les filles   les garçons

5. **(grand)** _____

_____

les girafes   les cochons

6. **(gros)** _____

_____

Les comparaisons

Nom_____

You can compare things that are equal by using the expression:

aussi + adjective + que

(as _____ as)

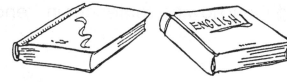

exemple: L'espagnol est **aussi** important **que** l'anglais.

(Spanish is as important as English.)

Tell that the two people or items mentioned are equal in the given quality.

1. **le chien – le chat/antipathique**

_____

2. **Suzanne – Julie/joli**

_____

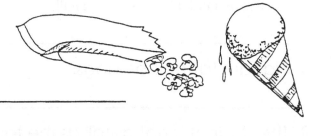

3. **le popcorn – la glace/délicieux**

_____

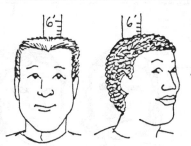

4. **Claude– Xavier/grand**

_____

5. **la maison #1 – la maison #2/grand**

_____

_____

Les comparaisons – pratique

Nom_____

Practice all three types of comparisons by writing the following sentences in French.

1. Cars are larger than bicycles.

_____

2. Fathers are as smart as mothers.

_____

3. School is less interesting than the beach.

_____

4. Jean is as nice as Estèle.

_____

5. My house is smaller than my school.

_____

6. André is taller than his brother.

_____

7. Tennis is as fun as volleyball.

_____

8. Pigs are fatter than dogs.

_____

9. The student is not as tall as the teacher.

_____

10. Suzanne is not as pretty as my mother.

_____

11. The cat is not as mean as the bird.

_____

12. The chair is not bigger than the refrigerator.

_____

Combien ça coûte?

How much does it cost?

Nom _____

To ask how much something costs, the verb **coûter** is used with the question words **Combien ça . . .** You will only use two forms of the verb **coûter; coûte** (it costs) and **coûtent** (they cost).

exemples: Le livre coûte trente francs.
Deux livres coûtent soixante francs.

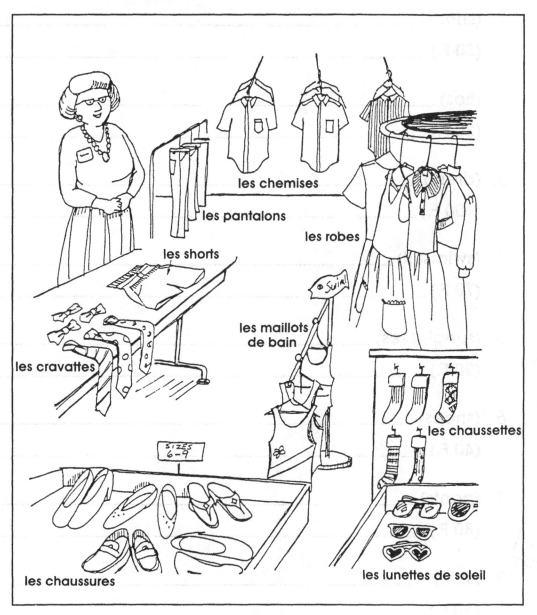

les chemises

les pantalons

les robes

les shorts

les maillots de bain

les cravattes

les chaussettes

SIZES 6-9

les chaussures

les lunettes de soleil

Combien ça coûte?

Nom_____

A sale is on at your favorite clothing store. Ask the salesperson how much each item in parentheses costs. Then write the response using the given price.

exemple: **(socks)** Combien coûtent les chausettes?

(10 F.) Elles coûtent dix francs.

1. **(shorts)** _____

(30 F.) _____

2. **(ties)** _____

(20 F.) _____

3. **(dress)** _____

(100 F.) _____

4. **(swimsuit)** _____

(70 F.) _____

5. **(sunglasses)** _____

(20 F.) _____

6. **(shoes)** _____

(40 F.) _____

7. **(pants)** _____

(80 F.) _____

8. **(shirt)** _____

(60 F.) _____

9. **(socks)** _____

(10 F.) _____

D'où viens-tu?
Where do you come from?

Nom_____

Venir			
je	**viens**	nous	**venons**
tu	**viens**	vous	**venez**
il	**vient**	ils	**viennent**
elle	**vient**	elles	**viennent**

The verb **venir** (to come) is irregular.

exemples: D'où viens-tu?

(Where do you come from?)

Je viens de la Bolivie.

(I come from Bolivia.)

Use the verb **parler** (to speak) with the name of the language spoken.

exemple: Je parle français.   (I speak French.)

Using the verb **venir**, tell where the following people come from and what language they speak.

France

1. **Claude**_____**du Mexique.**
   Il parle_____.

2. **Les filles**_____**de France.**
   Elles parlent_____.

3. **Nous**_____**du Japon.**
   Nous parlons_____.

4. **Françoise et Marcel**_____
   d'Italie.
   Ils parlent_____.

5. **Vous**_____**de Russie.**
   Vous parlez_____.

6. **Je**_____**d'Allemagne.**
   Je parle_____.

7. **Anne**_____**du Portugal.**
   Elle parle_____.

8. **Tu**_____**d'Angleterre.**
Tu parles_____.

Languages Spoken Around the World

l'espagnol	=	Spanish
l'anglais	=	English
le français	=	French
l'allemand	=	German
le russe	=	Russian
le portugais	=	Portuguese
l'italien	=	Italian
le japonais	=	Japanese
le chinois	=	Chinese

Il y a
There Is/There Are

Nom_____

Il y a is an expression meaning "there is" or "there are." It can be followed by a singular or a plural noun.

Qu'**y a**-t-**il** dans le réfrigérateur? (What is there in the refrigerator?)

Il y a du lait dans le réfrigérateur. (There's milk in the refrigerator.)

Combien d'enfants **y a**-t-**il** dans la classe? (How many children are there in the class?)

Il y a douze enfants dans la classe. (There are twelve children in the class.)

Combien de maisons **y a**-t-**il** dans la rue? (How many houses are there on the street?)

Il y a vingt maisons dans la rue. (There are twenty houses on the street.)

Note: Since **il y a** is a verbal expression, write **il n'y a pas** to make it negative.

Il n'y a pas de livres ici. (There are no books here./ There aren't any books here.)

Regardez les photos et écrivez les réponses.

1. **Combien de garçons y a-t-il dans la famille?**

   _____

2. **Combien de filles y a-t-il dans la famille?**

   _____

3. **Y a-t-il un père?**

   _____

4. **Y a-t-il une mère?**

   _____

1. **Y a-t-il des chiens?**

   _____

2. **Combien de chiens y a-t-il?**

   _____

3. **Combien de chats y a-t-il?**

   _____

4. **Combien d'oiseaux y a-t-il?**

Monique et Claude

Nom_____

Lisez les paragraphes et répondez aux questions.

Bonjour! Je m'apelle Monique Dulac. Je viens de France. Je suis l'amie de Claude Pelletier.

Claude vient des États-Unis. Il est formidable. Il est petit, blond, et franc. Il aime faire du sport. Moi aussi. Nous aimons le tennis et le foot-ball. Nous n'aimons pas nager ou courir.

Je suis étudiante dans un lycée de Dijon. Claude est étudiant dans un lycée de Lyons. J'aime l'histoire et surtout les mathématiques. Claude n'aime pas les mathématiques mais il aime l'histoire aussi. Nous sommes intelligents.

1. **Est-ce que Monique vient des États-Unis?**

   _____

2. **Est-ce que Claude vient d'Espagne?**

   _____

3. **Comment est Claude?**

   _____

4. **Est-ce que Claude aime faire du sport?**

   _____

5. **Est-ce que Monique aime faire du sport aussi?**

   _____

6. **Est-ce qu'ils aiment courrir?**

   _____

7. **Où est le lycée de Monique?**

   _____

8. **Où est le lycée de Claude?**

   _____

9. **Est-ce que Monique aime les mathématiques?**

   _____

10. **Sont-ils intelligents?**

    _____

Anita

Nom _____

Lisez les paragraphes et répondez aux questions. (Read the paragraphs and answer the questions.)

Anita vit à Santiago. Elle vient du Chili. Elle parle espagnol et français aussi. Elle aime le cours d'anglais au lycée. Elle est très intelligente mais elle n'aime pas le professeur de biologie. Elle aime porter une chemisette et un blue-jean au lycée. Elle aime chanter et danser.

1. **Où vit Anita?**

   _____

2. **Est-ce que Anita vient du Mexique?**

   _____

3. **Quelles classes plaisent à Anita?**

   _____

4. **Est-ce qu'elle aime aller au lycée?**

   _____

5. **Parle-t-elle français?**

   _____

Paul

Paul est très sportif. Il aime le football. Il est grand, blond et en pleine forme. Il vit à la campagne. Il travaille avec son oncle. Il aime la campagne. Il n'aime pas le lycée, les cours ou les professeurs. Il aime les étudiantes et, surtout, les jolies filles. Paul et ses amis écoutent la radio et regardent la télévision.

1. **Est-ce que Paul est sportif?**

   _____

2. **Est-ce que Paul est petit et brun?**

   _____

3. **Où vit Paul?**

   _____

4. **Est-ce qu'il étudie à la campagne?**

   _____

5. **Est-ce qu'il aime le lycée?**

   _____

Vocabulaire

Vocabulary

Nom_____

```
O C T D E C R A E S G P T L W C O C
T E E T E Y O L A G A R E A N H G A
N T L I H M E M E C H E G P T D R T
D H E F N A A A B O E O T O L L O N
C V P S T C U I S I N E R R E U S D
I W R H F N T L N F E O E T T S R A
S I I E E O S E I I E N U E E E D L
C N N O E O T O C E D H C R M N N X
O N T F I T S L L E M A N T E A U V
U L E E P A R E L T E O S T L A R I
R A M S L A R J E A D O S O E E E R
R N P I M G E O M A N I B D R E E N
I G S M S L R U U T R E I D E D B E
R L A E A R H E S T C R N M R Q T R
A A E E E T E T E B S O W A H T A R
E I H L N H A G E E P M G E K W A Y
N S L F T H A T L E T E O T K F N I
E A T R M B N T R N R H N E I G E R
```

Traduissez les mots et trouvez les mots en français.
(Translate the words and find the French translations.)

to go	to snow
train station	spring (season)
to answer	English
to look (at)	how many
tomorrow	sad
coat	fat
curtains	to cook
door	summer
toy	to run
thirst	museum

Révision

Nom_____

Write the following words in French.

1. to be _____
2. boring _____
3. to cry _____
4. easy _____
5. factory worker _____
6. cheese _____
7. to swim _____
8. journalist _____
9. lawyer _____
10. midnight _____

11. nurse _____
12. to play _____
13. to read _____
14. sad _____
15. sandals _____
16. shoes _____
17. sixty _____
18. tie _____
19. what _____
20. to work _____

Identifiez les vêtements sur les photos.

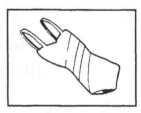

_____ _____ _____ _____

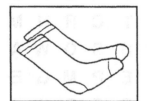

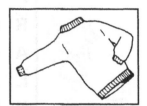

_____ _____ _____ _____

Écrivez les nombres.

1. cinquante _____
2. trois cents _____
3. mille _____
4. cinq cents _____
5. sept cents _____

6. soixante-douze _____
7. quatre-vingt onze _____
8. un million _____
9. quatre mille _____
10. soixante _____

Answer Key
French
Middle/High School

Salutations
Nom _____

Greet each of the following people in French.

1. your best friend — Salut!
2. your teacher — Bonjour!
3. your dad's boss — Bonjour!
4. your principal — Bonjour!
5. an unmarried lady — Bonjour, mademoiselle!
6. the mailman — Bonjour, monsieur!

Write the French words that are missing.

Salut

Bonjour

madame

Bonsoir

Bonjour, madame

Bonjour

Page 2

Comment ça va?
How are you?
Nom _____

Écrivez en français.

Comment ça va? (How are you?)
Comment ça va?

Très bien, merci. (Very well, thanks.)
Très bien, merci.

Ça va bien. (Fine, thanks.)
Ça va bien.

Comme ci comme ça. (So-so.)
Comme ci comme ça.

Mal. (Badly.)
Mal.

Très mal! (Very badly!)
Très mal!

Page 3

Comment ça va?
Nom _____

Define the following terms.

Comment ça va? — How are you? (How is it going?)
Ça va bien. — Fine. (It's going fine.)
Mal! — Badly!
Comme ci comme ça. — So so.
Très bien. — Very well.
Très mal. — Very badly.

Answer according to the pictures.

Très bien.

Mal.

Ça va bien.

Comme ci comme ça.

Très mal.

Page 4

Révision
Review

Nom_____

Finissez les phrases. (Complete with the appropriate words.)

monsieur · Comment · çi comme ça.

Salut · ça va · bien, merci.

Bonsoir · Comment · Très

madame · Comment ça va · Très bien

Page 5

Au revoir
Good-bye

Nom_____

Écrivez en français.

Au revoir. (Good-bye.)
Au revoir.

Adieu. (Formal goodbye.)
Adieu.

À tout à l'heure. (See you later.)
À tout à l'heure.

À demain. (See you tomorrow.)
À demain.

Écrivez en anglais. (Write what they are saying in English.)

Hi André! How are you?
Fine, thanks.

See you later.
Goodbye

Page 6

Comment t'appelles-tu?
What's your name?

Nom_____

In French there are two ways to ask "What's your name?" **Comment vous appellez-vous?** is more formal. It uses the word **vous**, a polite form of the word "you." **Vous** is usually used with someone you don't know very well or who is older than you.

The second way, **Comment t'appelles-tu?**, is less formal. It uses the word **tu**, a familiar form of the word "you." **Tu** is usually used with someone you know very well (a family member or close friend), someone younger than you, or a pet.

The answer, **Je m'appelle . . .** (My name . . .) is used to answer both styles of questions.

Écrivez en français.

Comment vous appellez-vous?   Je m'appelle . . .

Comment t'appelles-tu?   Je m'appelle . . .

Finissez les phrases. (Complete the sentences.)

Je m'appelle Christine. Comment t' appelles-tu ?
Je m 'appelle Pierre.

Je m'appelle Madame Payot. Comment vous appellez-vous
Je m'appelle Monsieur Portalis.

Je m'appelle Marie-Claire. Comment t'appelles-tu?
Je m'appelle _answers vary_ .

Page 7

Révision
Review

Nom_____

I. Write the French words to complete the dialogues.

Va   Très   tout à

Comment   appellez-vous   Je m'appelle

II. Greet the people below in French.

Salut, Zack!   Bonsoir, monsieur!   Bonsoir, madame!   Bonjour, monsieur

III. Now tell them each good-bye in different ways.
answers vary

Page 8

Les nombres
Numbers

Écrivez les nombres en français.

1	2	3
un	deux	trois
un	deux	trois

4	5	6
quatre	cinq	six
quatre	cinq	six

7	8	9
sept	huit	neuf
sept	huit	neuf

10	11	12
dix	onze	douze
dix	onze	douze

13	14	15
treize	quatorze	quinze
treize	quatorze	quinze

16	17	18
seize	dix-sept	dix-huit
seize	dix-sept	dix-huit

19	20	21
dix-neuf	vingt	vingt et un
dix-neuf	vingt	vingt et un

22	23	24
vingt-deux	vingt-trois	vingt-quatre
vingt-deux	vingt-trois	vingt-quatre

25	26	27
vingt-cinq	vingt-six	vingt-sept
vingt-cinq	vingt-six	vingt-sept

28	29	30
vingt-huit	vingt-neuf	trente
vingt-huit	vingt-neuf	trente

Les nombres

Écrivez les nombres en français.

31	32	33
trente et un	trente-deux	trente-trois
trente et un	trente-deux	trente-trois

34	35	36
trente-quatre	trente-cinq	trente-six
trente-quatre	trente-cinq	trente-six

37	38	39
trente-sept	trente-huit	trente-neuf
trente-sept	trente-huit	trente-neuf

40	41	42
quarante	quarante et un	quarante-deux
quarante	quarante et un	quarante-deux

43	44	45
quarante-trois	quarante-quatre	quarante-cinq
quarante-trois	quarante-quatre	quarante-cinq

46	47	48
quarante-six	quarante-sept	quarante-huit
quarante-six	quarante-sept	quarante-huit

49	50	51
quarante-neuf	cinquante	cinquante et un
quarante-neuf	cinquante	cinquante et un

52	53	54
cinquante-deux	cinquante-trois	cinquante-quatre
cinquante-deux	cinquante-trois	cinquante-quatre

55	56	57
cinquante-cinq	cinquante-six	cinquante-sept
cinquante-cinq	cinquante-six	cinquante-sept

58	59	60
cinquante-huit	cinquante-neuf	soixante
cinquante-huit	cinquante-neuf	soixante

Les nombres

Écrivez les nombres en français.

61	62	63
soixante et un	soixante-deux	soixante-trois
soixante et un	soixante-deux	soixante-trois

64	65	66
soixante-quatre	soixante-cinq	soixante-six
soixante-quatre	soixante-cinq	soixante-six

67	68	69
soixante-sept	soixante-huit	soixante-neuf
soixante-sept	soixante-huit	soixante-neuf

70	71	72
soixante-dix	soixante et onze	soixante-douze
soixante-dix	soixante et onze	soixante-douze

73	74	75
soixante-treize	soixante-quatorze	soixante-quinze
soixante-treize	soixante-quatorze	soixante-quinze

76	77	78
soixante-seize	soixante-dix-sept	soixante-dix-huit
soixante-seize	soixante-dix-sept	soixante-dix-huit

79	80	81
soixante-dix-neuf	quatre-vingt	quatre-vingt et un
soixante-dix-neuf	quatre-vingt	quatre-vingt et un

82	83	84
quatre-vingt-deux	quatre-vingt-trois	quatre-vingt-quatre
quatre-vingt-deux	quatre-vingt-trois	quatre-vingt-quatre

85	86	87
quatre-vingt-cinq	quatre-vingt-six	quatre-vingt-sept
quatre-vingt-cinq	quatre-vingt-six	quatre-vingt-sept

88	89	90
quatre-vingt-huit	quatre-vingt-neuf	quatre-vingt-dix
quatre-vingt-huit	quatre-vingt-neuf	quatre-vingt-dix

Les nombres

91	92	93
quatre-vingt-onze	quatre-vingt-douze	quatre-vingt-treize
quatre-vingt-onze	quatre-vingt-douze	quatre-vingt-treize

94	95	96
quatre-vingt-quatorze	quatre-vingt-quinze	quatre-vingt-seize
quatre-vingt-quatorze	quatre-vingt-quinze	quatre-vingt-seize

97	98	99
quatre-vingt-dix-sept	quatre-vingt-dix-huit	quatre-vingt-dix-neuf
quatre-vingt-dix-sept	quatre-vingt-dix-huit	quatre-vingt-dix-neuf

100	101	200
cent	cent un	deux cents
cent	cent un	deux cents

202	300	303
deux cent deux	trois cents	trois cent trois
deux cent deux	trois cents	trois cent trois

400	404	500
quatre cents	quatre cent quatre	cinq cents
quatre cents	quatre cent quatre	cinq cents

600	700	800
six cents	sept cents	huit cents
six cents	sept cents	huit cents

900	1,000	1,100
neuf cents	mille	mille cent
neuf cents	mille	mille cent

1,500	2,000	10,000
mille cinq cents	deux mille	dix mille
mille cinq cents	deux mille	dix mille

100,000	1,000,000	1,000,000,000
cent mille	un million	un milliard
cent mille	un million	un milliard

105   IF 8793 French

Les nombres

Nom _____

Écrivez les nombres en français.

1. 67 soixante-sept
2. 181 cent quatre-vingt et un
3. 92 quatre-vingt-douze
4. 74 soixante-quatorze
5. 243 deux cent quarante-trois
6. 515 cinq cent quinze
7. 926 neuf cent vingt-six
8. 304 trois cent quatre
9. 1,200 mille deux cent
10. 4,000 quatre mille

11. 500,126 cinq cent mille cent vingt-six
12. 1,894,037 un million huit cent mille quatre-vingt-dix mille quatre mille trente-sept
13. 3,600,012 trois million six cent mille douze
14. 987,651 neuf cent mille quatre-vingt mille sept mille six cent cinquante et un

Écrivez les nombres.

1. trois cent quatre-vingt-treize 393
2. quarante-huit 48
3. huit mille sept 8,007
4. mille cent un 1,101
5. sept cent treize 713
6. deux mille onze 2,011
7. un million quatorze 1,000,014
8. quatre-vingt deux 82
9. cinquante 50
10. quinze mille 15,000
11. mille neuf cent 1,900
12. trois mille 3,000
13. deux cent seize 216
14. trois milliards 3,000,000,000

Write how you would say the following years in French.

exemple: 1995 mille neuf cent quatre-vingt-quinze

1492 mille quatre cent quatre-vingt-douze
1776 mille sept cent soixante-seize
1955 mille neuf cent cinquante-cinq
1812 mille huit cent douze
1548 mille cinq cent quarante-huit
1637 mille six cent trente-sept

Les jours de la semaine
Days of the Week

Nom _____

lundi	mardi	mercredi	jeudi	vendredi	samedi	dimanche
	1	2	3	4	5	6
7	8	9	10	11	12	13
14	15	16	17	18	19	20
21	22	23	24	25	26	27
28	29	30	31			

Écrivez en français.

lundi (Monday) lundi
mardi (Tuesday) mardi
mercredi (Wednesday) mercredi
jeudi (Thursday) jeudi

vendredi (Friday) vendredi
samedi (Saturday) samedi
dimanche (Sunday) dimanche
le jour (day) le jour

I. Écrivez les jours de la semaine. (Note: In French Monday comes first.)

lundi, mardi, mercredi, jeudi, vendredi, samedi, dimanche

II. Écrivez le jour suivant. (Write the following day.)

mardi mercredi
dimanche lundi
jeudi vendredi
lundi mardi
vendredi samedi
samedi dimanche
mercredi jeudi

III. Écrivez en français. (Write in French.)

Sunday dimanche
Tuesday mardi
Wednesday mercredi
Monday lundi
Friday vendredi
Thursday jeudi
Saturday samedi

Les mois
Months of the Year

Nom _____

Écrivez les mois en français.

janvier janvier
février février
mars mars
avril avril

mai mai
juin juin
juillet juillet
août août

septembre septembre
octobre octobre
novembre novembre
décembre décembre

I. Écrivez le mois suivant. (Write the following month.)

mars avril
décembre janvier
juillet août
octobre novembre
février mars
juin juillet

janvier février
avril mai
août septembre
mai juin
septembre octobre
novembre décembre

II. Combien de jours y a-t-il dans chaque mois? Écrivez les nombres en français. (How many days are in each month? Write the numbers in French.)

juin trente
décembre trente et un
août trente et un
février vingt-huit or vingt-neuf

octobre trente et un
juillet trente et un
novembre trente
mai trente et un

Quelle est la date?
What is the date?

Nom _____

Quelle est la date aujourd'hui? (What is today's date?)
Aujourd'hui, c'est le onze avril. (Today is the 11th of April.)

Quelle est la date aujourd'hui?
Aujourd'hui, c'est le premier septembre. (Today is September 1st.)

Écrivez les dates en français.

Quelle est la date aujourd'hui?
Aujourd'hui, c'est le trois février.

Quelle est la date aujourd'hui?
Aujourd'hui, c'est le vingt-cinq décembre.

Quelle est la date aujourd'hui?
Aujourd'hui, c'est le deux janvier.

Quelle est la date ...

aujourd'hui? answers vary
demain? (tomorrow) answers vary
de ton anniversaire? (your birthday) answers vary
de Noël? (Christmas) C'est le vingt-cinq décembre
du jour d'indépendance? (Independence Day) answers vary
du premier jour d'école? (the first day of school) answers vary
du réveillon? (New Year's Eve) C'est le trente et un décembre

J'aime . . .
I like . . .

Nom_____

Écrivez les phrases en français.
(Write the sentences in French.)

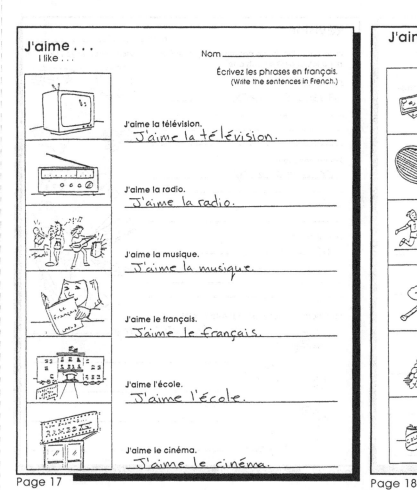

J'aime la télévision.
J'aime la télévision.

J'aime la radio.
J'aime la radio.

J'aime la musique.
J'aime la musique.

J'aime le français.
J'aime le français.

J'aime l'école.
J'aime l'école.

J'aime le cinéma.
J'aime le cinéma.

Page 17

J'aime . . .

Nom_____

Écrivez les phrases en français.

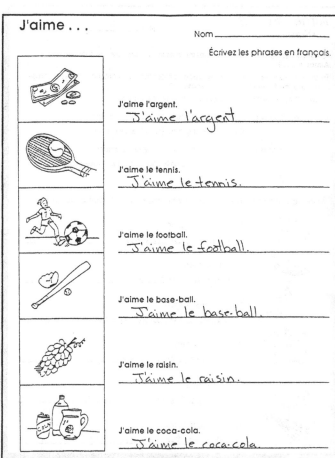

J'aime l'argent.
J'aime l'argent

J'aime le tennis.
J'aime le tennis.

J'aime le football.
J'aime le football.

J'aime le base-ball.
J'aime le base-ball.

J'aime le raisin.
J'aime le raisin.

J'aime le coca-cola.
J'aime le coca-cola.

Page 18

J'aime beaucoup . . .
I really like . . .

Nom_____

Écrivez les phrases en français.

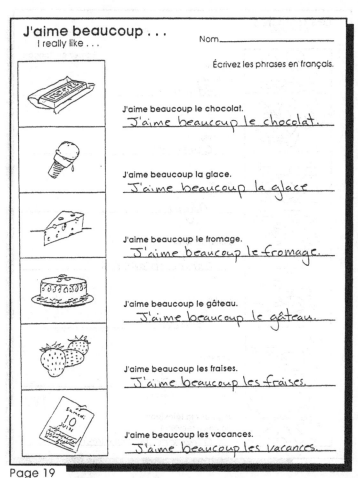

J'aime beaucoup le chocolat.
J'aime beaucoup le chocolat.

J'aime beaucoup la glace.
J'aime beaucoup la glace

J'aime beaucoup le fromage.
J'aime beaucoup le fromage.

J'aime beaucoup le gâteau.
J'aime beaucoup le gâteau.

J'aime beaucoup les fraises.
J'aime beaucoup les fraises.

J'aime beaucoup les vacances.
J'aime beaucoup les vacances.

Page 19

Je n'aime pas . . .
I don't like . . .

Nom_____

Écrivez les phrases en français.

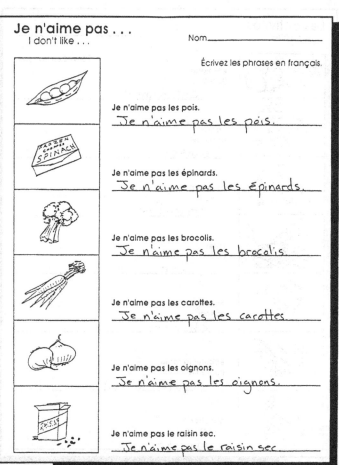

Je n'aime pas les pois.
Je n'aime pas les pois.

Je n'aime pas les épinards.
Je n'aime pas les épinards.

Je n'aime pas les brocolis.
Je n'aime pas les brocolis.

Je n'aime pas les carottes.
Je n'aime pas les carottes

Je n'aime pas les oignons.
Je n'aime pas les oignons.

Je n'aime pas le raisin sec.
Je n'aime pas le raisin sec

Page 20

Aimes-tu . . . ?
Do you like . . . ?

Nom_____

To ask someone you know well if he/she likes something, use the **familiar** form, **Aimes-tu . . . ?**

To ask someone you do not know well or is older than you are if he/she likes something, use the **formal** form, **Aimez-vous . . . ?**

Answer these questions with "**J'aime . . .**" or "**Je n'aime pas . . .**"

Exemple: (familiar) Aimes-tu la glace? (Do you like ice cream?)

Oui, j'aime la glace. (Yes, I like ice cream.)

(formal) Aimez-vous le raisin? (Do you like grapes?)

Non, je n'aime pas le raisin. (No, I don't like grapes.)

Write a question asking each person what they think of each pictured item.

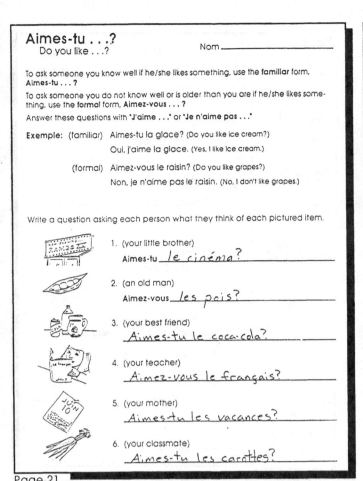

1. (your little brother)
   Aimes-tu _le cinéma?_

2. (an old man)
   Aimez-vous _les pois?_

3. (your best friend)
   Aimes-tu le coca-cola?

4. (your teacher)
   Aimez-vous le français?

5. (your mother)
   Aimes-tu les vacances?

6. (your classmate)
   Aimes-tu les carottes?

Page 21

Révision

Nom_____

Write each item in the correct category in French to show whether you like, like a lot, or dislike each one.

J'aime . . .
answers vary

J'aime beaucoup . . .
answers vary

Je n'aime pas . . .
answers vary

Tell whether or not you like the items pictured.

answers vary

Page 22

Les activités
Activities

Nom_____

Écrivez en français.

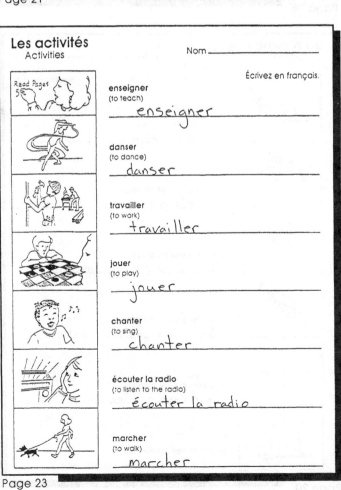

enseigner
(to teach)
enseigner

danser
(to dance)
danser

travailler
(to work)
travailler

jouer
(to play)
jouer

chanter
(to sing)
chanter

écouter la radio
(to listen to the radio)
écouter la radio

marcher
(to walk)
marcher

Page 23

Les activités
Activities

Nom_____

Écrivez en français.

étudier
(to study)
étudier

cuisiner
(to cook)
cuisiner

nager
(to swim)
nager

parler français
(to speak French)
parler français

sauter
(to jump)
sauter

acheter
(to buy)
acheter

regarder la télévision
(to watch television)
regarder la télévision

Page 24

IF8793 French

Les activités

Nom_____

Tell whether you **like**, **like a lot**, or **do not like** to do the activities in each picture.

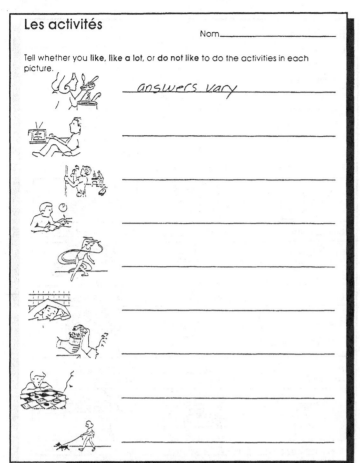

_answers vary_____

_____

_____

_____

_____

_____

_____

_____

Page 25

Et toi?
And you?

Nom_____

Répondez en français. (Answer in French.)

J'aime la musique
Je n'aime pas la musique

J'aime nager
Je n'aime pas nager.

J'aime la glace.
Je n'aime pas la glace

J'aime le coca-cola.
Je n'aime pas le coca-cola.

Page 26

Les verbes en -er
-Er Verbs

Nom _____

You have learned how to speak in French about what you like and do not like to do. It is also useful to be able to tell what you and other people do.

Most verbs in French end in **-er** (chanter = to sing, travailler = to work, nager = to swim). This form of the verb is called the infinitive.

The **stem** of the verb is the infinitive minus the **-er** (example: parler–er = parl). Different endings are added to the stem for each subject.

Here are the subject pronouns and the endings for each one for the sample verb **parler**.

Parler					
Singular			Plural		
I	je	parle	we	nous	parlons
you (fam.)	tu	parles			
you (formal)	vous	parlez	you (pl.)	vous	parlez
			they	ils/elles	parlent
he/she	il/elle	parle			

Study the list of verbs below.

parler	= to speak	jouer	= to play
chanter	= to sing	visiter	= to visit
nager	= to swim	téléphoner	= to telephone
écouter	= to listen (to)	regarder	= to look (at)
danser	= to dance	porter	= to wear
étudier	= to study	donner	= to give
		sauter	= to jump

acheter = to buy
travailler = to work
préparer = to prepare
marcher = to walk
désirer = to want
adorer = to adore
pleurer = to cry

Page 27

Les verbes en -er

Nom_____

I. Write the stems of the verbs below.

étudier __étudi__   travailler __travaill__   sauter __saut__

nager __nag__   donner __donn__   acheter __achet__

écouter __écout__   marcher __march__   porter __port__

chanter __chant__   regarder __regard__   téléphoner __téléphon__

II. Write the **-er** endings for each of the subject pronouns below.

tu __-es__   je __-e__   ils __-ent__

il __-e__   nous __-ons__   elles __-ent__

vous __-ez__   elle __-e__

III. Write the correct form for each subject for the verbs below.

chanter   stem __chant__

je __chante__   il __chante__   vous __chantez__

tu __chantes__   nous __chantons__   ils __chantent__

étudier   stem __étudi__

je j'__étudie__   elle __étudie__   vous __étudiez__

tu __étudies__   nous __étudions__   elles __étudient__

porter   stem __port__

je __porte__   il __porte__   vous __portez__

tu __portes__   nous __portons__   elles __portent__

Page 28

Les verbes en -er

Nom _____

Use the pictures to write and conjugate the verbs.

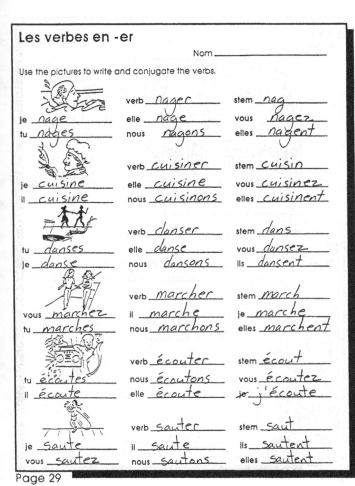

verb _nager_   stem _nag_
je _nage_   elle _nage_   vous _nagez_
tu _nages_   nous _nageons_   elles _nagent_

verb _cuisiner_   stem _cuisin_
je _cuisine_   elle _cuisine_   vous _cuisinez_
il _cuisine_   nous _cuisinons_   elles _cuisinent_

verb _danser_   stem _dans_
tu _danses_   elle _danse_   vous _dansez_
je _danse_   nous _dansons_   ils _dansent_

verb _marcher_   stem _march_
vous _marchez_   il _marche_   je _marche_
tu _marches_   nous _marchons_   elles _marchent_

verb _écouter_   stem _écout_
tu _écoutes_   nous _écoutons_   vous _écoutez_
il _écoute_   elle _écoute_   je _j'écoute_

verb _sauter_   stem _saut_
je _saute_   il _saute_   ils _sautent_
vous _sautez_   nous _sautons_   elles _sautent_

Page 29

Révision

Nom _____

I. Matching.

1. I sing.	_1_ Je chante.
2. He dances.	_5_ Elle écoute.
3. They talk.	_7_ Nous travaillons.
4. You jump (fam.).	_4_ Tu sautes.
5. She listens.	_6_ Vous regardez.
6. You look (formal).	_3_ Ils parlent.
7. We work.	_2_ Il danse.

II. Fill in the blank with the appropriate verb form.

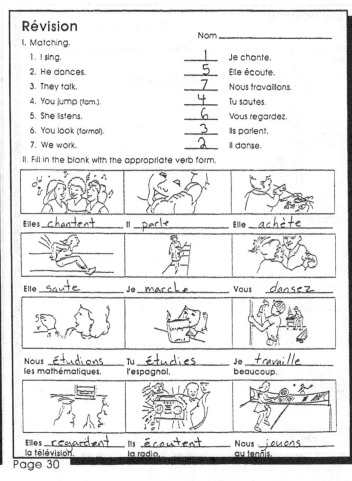

Elles _chantent_   Il _parle_   Elle _achète_

Elle _saute_   Je _marche_   Vous _dansez_

Nous _étudions_ les mathématiques.   Tu _étudies_ l'espagnol.   Je _travaille_ beaucoup.

Elles _regardent_ la télévision.   Ils _écoutent_ la radio.   Nous _jouons_ au tennis.

Page 30

Les vêtements
Clothing

Nom _____

Écrivez les mots en français.

le manteau	le short	le pullover	la robe
la jupe	la cravate	la chemise	les chaussures
les chaussettes	les sandales	le maillot de bain	le blouson

Écrivez les phrases en français.

1. I like T-shirts.
   J'aime les tee-shirts.
2. Martin is wearing shorts.
   Martin porte un short.
3. Anne and Marie wear dresses.
   Anne et Marie portent des robes.
4. We're wearing swimming suits.
   Nous portons des maillots de bain.
5. I'm buying a tie.
   J'achète une cravate

6. Do you like to wear sandals?
   Aimez-vous porter des sanda
7. They're buying skirts.
   Elles achètent des jupes.
8. She's buying the coat.
   Elle achète le manteau.
9. I like sweaters.
   J'aime les pullovers.
10. He's wearing a jacket.
   Il porte un blouson.

Page 31

Les questions
The Questions

Nom _____

One way to form a yes/no question in French is to reverse the order of the subject and the verb. Place a hyphen between the verb and the subject.

Exemple: Parles-tu français?

    (verb)   (subject)

*Remember that a question asked of you (addressed as tu or vous) should be answered with I (je). A question asked of you plural (vous) should be answered with we (nous). When the subject begins with a vowel and the verb also ends with a vowel, place a t between the subject and the verb.

    Parle-t-il français? (Does he speak French?)
    Oui, il parle français. (Yes, he speaks French.)

    Parlez-vous français? (Do you (plural) speak French?)
    Oui, nous parlons français. (Yes, we speak French.)

Répondez aux questions en français.
(Answer the questions in French.)

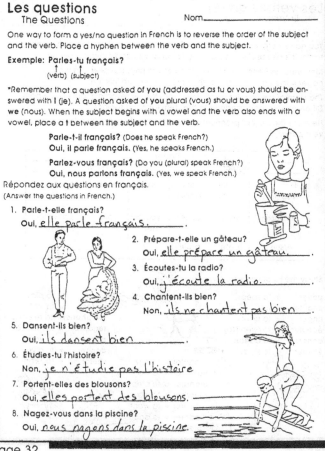

1. Parle-t-elle français?
   Oui, _elle parle français._
2. Prépare-t-elle un gâteau?
   Oui, _elle prépare un gâteau._
3. Écoutes-tu la radio?
   Oui, _j'écoute la radio._
4. Chantent-ils bien?
   Non, _ils ne chantent pas bien_
5. Dansent-ils bien?
   Oui, _ils dansent bien_
6. Études-tu l'histoire?
   Non, _je n'étudie pas l'histoire_
7. Portent-elles des blousons?
   Oui, _elles portent des blousons._
8. Nagez-vous dans la piscine?
   Oui, _nous nageons dans la piscine._

Page 32

   110

Les questions

Nom _____

Écrivez les questions.
(Write the questions.)

1. _Nage-t-elle bien?_ ?
   Non, elle ne nage pas bien.

2. _Chantez-vous_ ?
   Oui, nous chantons.

3. _Parle-t-il français_ ?
   Non, il ne parle pas français.

4. _Écoutent-ils la radio_ ?
   Oui, ils écoutent la radio.

5. _Joues-tu_ _Jouez-vous de la guitare?_
   Non, je ne joue pas de la guitare.

6. _Visitez-vous la France_ ?
   Oui, nous visitons la France.

7. _Porte-t-elle de manteau_ ?
   Non, elle ne porte pas de manteau.

8. _Étudies-tu_ _Étudiez-vous les sciences_ ?
   Oui, j'étudie les sciences (science).

9. _Dansent-ils_ ?
   Non, ils ne dansent pas.

10. _Parles-tu_ _Parlez-vous français_ ?
    Oui, je parle français.

11. _Regarde-t-il la télévision_ ?
    Non, il ne regarde pas la télévision.

12. _Chantez-vous_ ?
    Oui, nous chantons.

13. _Écoute-t-elle la musique_ ?
    Oui, elle écoute la musique.

Salut!

Les négations
Negatives

Nom _____

To make a sentence negative, simply put the word **ne** before the verb and the word **pas** after the verb.

exemple: Je parle français. (I speak French.)
Je ne parle pas français. (I do not speak French.)

Make each sentence negative.

Ils sautent.
Ils ne sautent pas.

Elles nagent.
Elles ne nagent pas.

Il marche.
Il ne marche pas

Je regarde la télévision.
Je ne regarde pas la télévision

Nous dansons.
Nous ne dansons pas.

Elle étudie.
Elle n'étudie pas.

Les questions

Nom _____

Répondez aux questions.
Answer the questions.

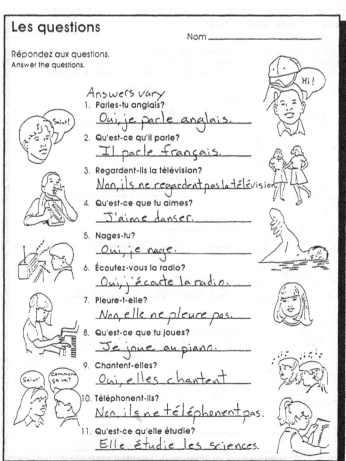

Answers vary

1. Parles-tu anglais?
   Oui, je parle anglais.

2. Qu'est-ce qu'il parle?
   Il parle français.

3. Regardent-ils la télévision?
   Non, ils ne regardent pas la télévision

4. Qu'est-ce que tu aimes?
   J'aime danser.

5. Nages-tu?
   Oui, je nage.

6. Écoutez-vous la radio?
   Oui, j'écoute la radio.

7. Pleure-t-elle?
   Non, elle ne pleure pas.

8. Qu'est-ce que tu joues?
   Je joue au piano.

9. Chantent-elles?
   Oui, elles chantent

10. Téléphonent-ils?
    Non, ils ne téléphonent pas.

11. Qu'est-ce qu'elle étudie?
    Elle étudie les sciences.

Qu'est-ce que ça veut dire?
What does that mean?

Nom _____

Write the meanings of the questions and answers below in English.

Dansez-vous?
Are you dancing?
Oui, nous dansons beaucoup.
Yes, we're dancing a lot.
Regardes-tu la télévision?
Are you watching television?
Oui, je regarde la télévision.
Yes, I'm watching television.
Sautent-elles?
Are they jumping?
Oui, elles sautent.
Yes, they are jumping.
Travaillent-ils?
Are they working?
Oui, ils travaillent.
Yes, they are working.
Nage-t-elle?
Is she swimming?
Oui, elle nage.
Yes, she is swimming.
Chantes-tu bien?
Are you singing well?
Oui, je chante bien.
Yes, I'm singing well

Answering Questions Negatively

Nom_____

Respond to the following questions negatively.

exemple: Danses-tu? (Do you dance?)

Non, je ne danse pas. (No, I do not dance.)

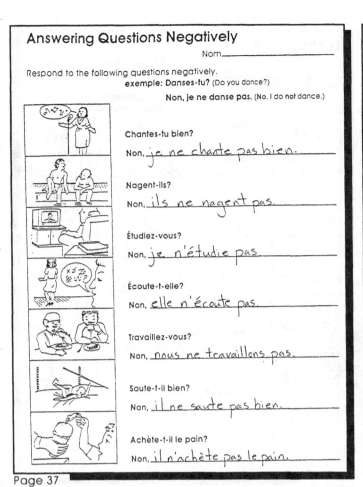

Chantes-tu bien?

Non, je ne chante pas bien.

Nagent-ils?

Non, ils ne nagent pas.

Étudiez-vous?

Non, je n'étudie pas.

Écoute-t-elle?

Non, elle n'écoute pas.

Travaillez-vous?

Non, nous ne travaillons pas.

Saute-t-il bien?

Non, il ne saute pas bien.

Achète-t-il le pain?

Non, il n'achète pas le pain.

Les questions
Questions

Nom_____

Answer the questions using the information in the pictures.

Écoute-t-elle la radio?

Oui, elle écoute la radio.

Regarde-t-elle la télévision?

Non, elle ne regarde pas la télévis

Travaille-t-il?

Oui, il travaille.

Danse-t-il?

Non, il ne danse pas.

Chantent-ils?

Oui, ils chantent.

Nagent-ils?

Non, ils ne nagent pas.

Parlez-vous français?

Oui, nous parlons français.

Parlez-vous anglais?

Non, nous ne parlons pas anglais.

Regarde-t-il?

Oui, il regarde.

Saute-t-il?

Non, il ne saute pas.

Achète-t-elle une chemise?

Oui, elle achète une chemise.

Achète-t-elle de la glace?

Non, elle n'achète pas de glace.

Qu'est-ce que c'est?
What is it?

Nom_____

Qu'est-ce que c'est?
(What is it?)

C'est une voiture.
(It's a car.)

Qu'est-ce que c'est?
(What is it?)

C'est une pomme.
(It's an apple.)

Un and **une** are **indefinite articles**. They are the equivalent of "a" or "an" in English. **Un** is used with **masculine** and **une** is used with **feminine** nouns.

Use **un** and **une** with nouns you have already learned in this book.

Qu'est-ce que c'est?
C'est une glace.

Qu'est-ce que c'est?
C'est un gâteau.

Qu'est-ce que c'est?
C'est une fraise.

Qu'est-ce que c'est?
C'est un coca-cola.

Qu'est-ce que c'est?
C'est { un lycée.
        { une école.

Qu'est-ce que c'est?
What is it?

Nom_____

If there are several things in your answer, you will need the plural of the indefinite articles. The plural of **un** is **des**. The plural of **une** is **des**. **Des** means "some." Sometimes we leave out the word "some" in English, but it cannot be omitted in French.

Use **des** to identify some other nouns you have learned.

Exemple:

Qu'est-ce que c'est? (What are they?)

Ce sont des fraises. (They are (some) strawberries.)

Qu'est-ce que c'est?
C'est du raisin.

Qu'est-ce que c'est?
Ce sont des glaces.

Qu'est-ce que c'est?
Ce sont des coca-colas

Qu'est-ce que c'est?
Ce sont des oignons

Qu'est-ce que c'est?
Ce sont des chocolats.

Qu'est-ce que c'est?
Ce sont des fraises.

Qu'est-ce que . . . ?
What?
Nom _____

Qu'est-ce que are the words used to mean what. . . To form a question using Qu'est-ce que follow this pattern: **Qu'est-ce que + subject + verb?** The answer to this type of question will always be an object or an activity, a noun.

exemple 1: Qu'est-ce que tu achètes? (What are you buying?)

(object) J'achète **une chemise.** (I'm buying a shirt.)

exemple 2: Qu'est-ce qu'elle fait? (What is she doing?)

(activity) Elle **nage.** (She's swimming.)

Use the pictures to answer the following questions in French.

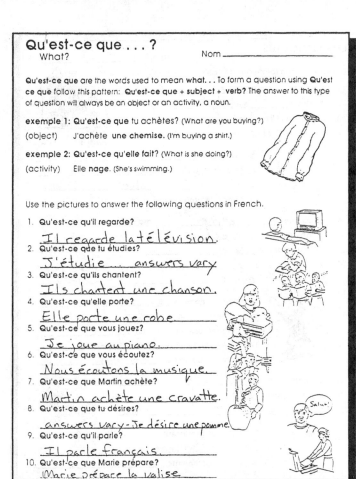

1. Qu'est-ce qu'il regarde?
   Il regarde la télévision.
2. Qu'est-ce que tu étudies?
   J'étudie . . . answers vary
3. Qu'est-ce qu'ils chantent?
   Ils chantent une chanson.
4. Qu'est-ce qu'elle porte?
   Elle porte une robe.
5. Qu'est-ce que vous jouez?
   Je joue au piano.
6. Qu'est-ce que vous écoutez?
   Nous écoutons la musique.
7. Qu'est-ce que Martin achète?
   Martin achète une cravatte.
8. Qu'est-ce que tu désires?
   answers vary - Je désire une pomme.
9. Qu'est-ce qu'il parle?
   Il parle français.
10. Qu'est-ce que Marie prépare?
    Marie prépare la valise.

Page 41

Les questions
Nom _____

Écrivez les questions avec **Qu'est-ce que . . .**
(Write the questions using **Qu'est-ce que . . .**)

1. _Qu'est-ce que tu aimes?_
   J'aime la glace.
2. _Qu'est-ce qu'il parle_ ?
   Il parle anglais.
3. _Qu'est-ce que tu portes_ ?
   Je porte un pantalon.
4. _Qu'est-ce que vous jouez_ ?
   Nous jouons du piano.
5. _Qu'est-ce que tu étudies_ ?
   J'étudie l'histoire.
6. _Qu'est-ce que vous visitez?_
   Nous visitons la France.
7. _Qu'est-ce qu'il écoute_ ?
   Il écoute la radio.
8. _Qu'est-ce qu'elles chantent?_
   Elles chantent la chanson.
9. _Qu'est-ce que tu regardes_ ?
   Je regarde la télévision.
10. _Qu'est-ce qu'elles répondent?_
    Elles répondent aux questions.
11. _Qu'est-ce que tu aimes_ ?
    J'aime le français.
12. _Qu'est-ce qu'elle étudies_ ?
    Elle étudie l'espagnol.
13. _Qu'est-ce que vous achetez?_
    Nous achetons le pain.

Le français

Page 42

Les adjectifs
Adjectives
Nom _____

An **adjective** is a word that describes a noun. In French all **nouns have gender.** They are either masculine or feminine. Each adjective **must agree** with the **gender** of the noun it describes. So adjectives in French have both masculine and feminine forms. Use the form that agrees with the gender of the noun.

Singular feminine adjectives often end in **-e.** Singular masculine ones often do not. Since singular feminine adjectives end in **-e,** the final consonant is pronounced. It is not pronounced in singular masculine adjectives.

The adjectives below are masculine. Make them feminine.

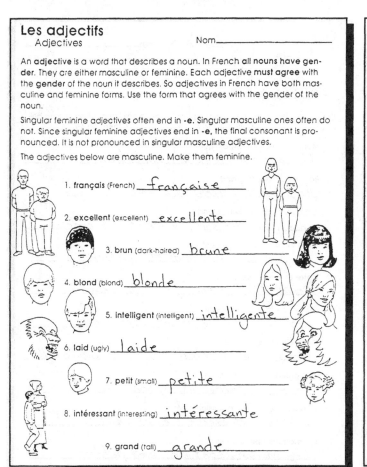

1. français (French) _française_
2. excellent (excellent) _excellente_
3. brun (dark-haired) _brune_
4. blond (blond) _blonde_
5. intelligent (intelligent) _intelligente_
6. laid (ugly) _laide_
7. petit (small) _petite_
8. intéressant (interesting) _intéressante_
9. grand (tall) _grande_

Page 43

Les adjectifs
Nom _____

Adjectives in French must agree in **number** as well as **gender.** That is, if the noun is singular, then the adjective describing it must also be singular. If the noun is plural, then the adjective must also be plural.

To make an adjective plural . . .

1. add -s

exemple: grand > grands

Most adjectives have four forms:

	singular	plural
masculine	grand	grands
feminine	grande	grandes

If a group contains both masculine and feminine nouns, use the masculine plural form.

exemple: Les garçons et les filles sont grands.
(The boys and the girls are tall.)

Fill in the blanks with the correct form of the underlined adjective in each phrase. **Remember:** Some adjectives change form because of gender.

1. small girls = les _petites_ filles
2. interesting books = les livres _intéressants_
3. blond men = les hommes _blonds_
4. intelligent people = les gens _intelligents_
5. French tests = les examens _français_
6. interesting classes = les classes _intéressantes_
7. pretty women = les _jolies_ femmes
8. intelligent teachers = les professeurs _intelligents_
9. ugly houses = les maisons _laides_
10. big trees = les _grands_ arbres
11. French boys = les garçons _français_
12. excellent fathers = les pères _excellents_

Page 44

© Instructional Fair • TS Denison | 113 | IF 8793 French

Les adjectifs

Nom_____

There are many adjectives that end in -e. These keep the same spelling no matter with which type of singular noun, masculine or feminine, they are used.

exemple: une fille **modeste**   un garçon **modeste**

Several adjectives of this type are . . .

modeste = modest	pauvre = poor	sévère = strict
célèbre = famous	stupide = stupid	difficile = hard
bête = dumb/stupid	riche = rich	triste = sad
irrésistible = irresistible	facile = easy	timide = shy
formidable = great	jeune = young	sympathique = nice
optimiste = optimistic	pessimiste = pessimistic	

Write the correct forms of the adjectives below.

1. an irresistible boy = un garçon _irrésistible_
2. a great car = une voiture _formidable_
3. a famous woman = une femme _célèbre_
4. a nice man = un homme _sympathique_
5. a stupid animal = un animal _bête_
6. a sad girl = une fille _triste_
7. an easy test = un examen _facile_
8. a rich man = un homme _riche_
9. an optimistic woman = une femme _optimiste_
10. a young student = un étudiant _jeune_
11. a great book = un livre _formidable_
12. a shy boy = un garçon _timide_
13. a strict father = un père _sévère_
14. an easy question = une question _facile_
15. a hard test = un examen _difficile_
16. a sad brother = un frère _triste_

Les adjectifs

Nom_____

Écrivez la bonne forme des adjectifs.

1. (big) une _grande_ maison
2. (short) un _petit_ homme
3. (blond) une fille _blonde_
4. (dark-haired) les hommes _bruns_
5. (small) une _petite_ classe
6. (excellent) un livre _excellent_
7. (pretty) les _jolies_ filles
8. (funny) le professeur _amusant_
9. (small) une _petite_ maison
10. (mean) le chien _méchant_
11. (ugly) un monstre _laid_
12. (tall) un _grand_ éléphant
13. (thin) un garçon _mince_
14. (nice) un homme _sympathique_
15. (perfect) un jour _parfait_
16. (elegant) une femme _élégante_
17. (intelligent) une fille _intelligente_
18. (content) un garçon _content_
19. (patient) une tortue _patiente_
20. (smart) un lapin _intelligent_
21. (big) un _grand_ animal
22. (nice) un professeur _sympathique_
23. (tall) les _grandes_ filles
24. (blond) un homme _blond_

Page 46

Être
To be

Nom_____

The verb **être** (to be) is used with adjectives to describe people or things. The verb **être** does not follow a regular pattern like the -er verbs. It is an irregular verb.

Être			
je	suis	nous	sommes
tu	es	vous	êtes
il	est	ils	sont
elle	est	elles	sont

Conjugate the verb **être** with the adjective **grand**. (The adjective must also agree with the subject.

1. Je (masc.) _suis_ _grand_
2. Tu _es_ _grand(e)_
3. Vous (sing.) _êtes_ _grand(e)_
4. Il _est_ _grand_
5. Elle _est_ _grande_
6. Nous _sommes_ _grand(e)s_
7. Je (fem.) _suis_ _grande_
8. Vous (pl.) _êtes_ _grand(e)s_
9. Ils _sont_ _grands_
10. Elles _sont_ _grandes_

Conjugate the verb **être** with the following adjectives.

petit (short)

1. Je (masc.) _suis_ _petit_
2. Tu (masc.) _es_ _petit_
3. Elle _est_ _petite_
4. Nous _sommes_ _petit(e)s_
5. Ils _sont_ _petits_
6. Vous (sing.) _êtes_ _petit(e)_

intelligent (intelligent)

1. Tu _es_ _intelligent(e)_
2. Elles _sont_ _intelligentes_
3. Nous _sommes_ _intelligent(e)s_
4. Je (fem.) _suis_ _intelligente_
5. Vous (sing.) _êtes_ _intelligent(e)_
6. Il _est_ _intelligent_
7. Ils _sont_ _intelligents_
8. Vous (pl.) _êtes_ _intelligent(e)s_

Page 47

Être

Nom_____

Use the adjectives to describe the people and things listed. All adjectives are given in the masculine singular form. Be sure to make them agree!

1. Monique – riche, sympathique
   Monique est riche et sympathique.
2. Robert – innocent, grand
   Robert est innocent et grand.
3. Anne et Marie – patient, blond
   Anne et Marie sont patientes et blondes.
4. Marc et Paul – laid, impatient
   Marc et Paul sont laids et impatients.
5. Pierre et Sylvie – petit, brun
   Pierre et Sylvie sont petits et bruns.
6. Les livres – facile, intéressant
   Les livres sont faciles et intéressants.
7. Nous – intelligent, beau
   Nous sommes intelligent(e)s et beaux/belles.
8. Je – grand, sympathique
   Je suis grande et sympathique.
9. Le repas – excellent, abondant
   Le repas est excellent et abondant.
10. Les maisons – beau, petit
    Les maisons sont beaux et petites.

Page 48

© Instructional Fair • TS Denison   114   IF8793 French

Les questions avec le verbe être

Nom _____

Répondez aux questions. (Answer the questions.)
Use the pictures as clues for your answers.

exemple: **Est-ce que Michel est riche?**

Oui, il est riche.

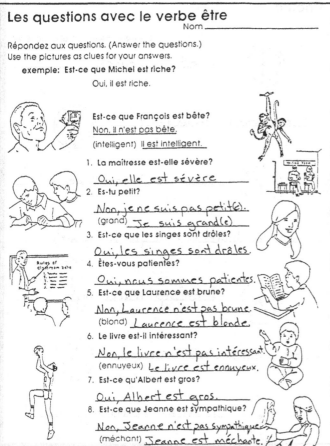

Est-ce que François est bête?
Non, il n'est pas bête.
(intelligent) Il est intelligent.

1. La maîtresse est-elle sévère?
Oui, elle est sévère

2. Es-tu petit?
Non, je ne suis pas petit(e).
(grand) _Je suis grand(e)_

3. Est-ce que les singes sont drôles?
Oui, les singes sont drôles.

4. Êtes-vous patientes?
Oui, nous sommes patientes.

5. Est-ce que Laurence est brune?
Non, Laurence n'est pas brune.
(blond) _Laurence est blonde._

6. Le livre est-il intéressant?
Non, le livre n'est pas intéressant.
(ennuyeux) _Le livre est ennuyeux._

7. Est-ce qu'Albert est gros?
Oui, Albert est gros.

8. Est-ce que Jeanne est sympathique?
Non, Jeanne n'est pas sympathique.
(méchant) _Jeanne est méchante._

Page 49

Les professions
Professions

Nom _____

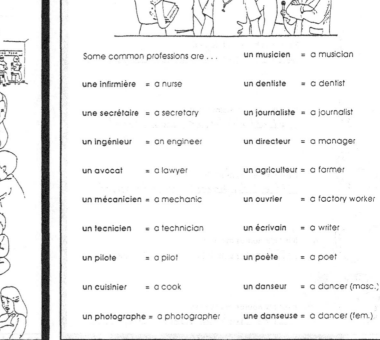

Some common professions are . . .

		un musicien	= a musician
une infirmière	= a nurse	un dentiste	= a dentist
une secrétaire	= a secretary	un journaliste	= a journalist
un ingénieur	= an engineer	un directeur	= a manager
un avocat	= a lawyer	un agriculteur	= a farmer
un mécanicien	= a mechanic	un ouvrier	= a factory worker
un tecnicien	= a technician	un écrivain	= a writer
un pilote	= a pilot	un poète	= a poet
un cuisinier	= a cook	un danseur	= a dancer (masc.)
un photographe	= a photographer	une danseuse	= a dancer (fem.)

Page 50

Les professions

Nom _____

Indefinite articles (un, une) are not used with the professions after the verb être unless they are modified by an adjective.

exemples: Colette est chanteuse. (Colette is a singer.)

Colette est une bonne chanteuse. (Colette is a good singer.)

Fill in the blanks with the correct form of être and the indicated professions.

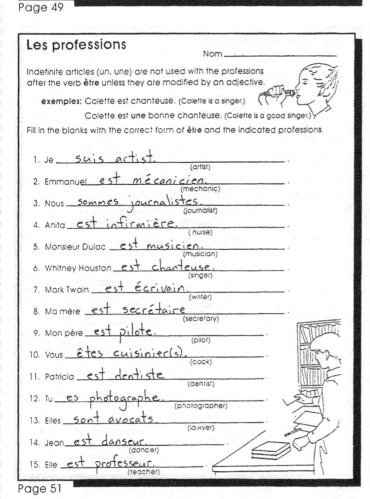

1. Je _suis artist._
(artist)

2. Emmanuel _est mécanicien._
(mechanic)

3. Nous _sommes journalistes._
(journalist)

4. Anita _est infirmière._
(nurse)

5. Monsieur Dulac _est musicien._
(musician)

6. Whitney Houston _est chanteuse._
(singer)

7. Mark Twain _est écrivain._
(writer)

8. Ma mère _est secrétaire._
(secretary)

9. Mon père _est pilote._
(pilot)

10. Vous _êtes cuisinier(s)._
(cook)

11. Patricia _est dentiste._
(dentist)

12. Tu _es photographe._
(photographer)

13. Elles _sont avocats_
(lawyer)

14. Jean _est danseur._
(dancer)

15. Elle _est professeur._
(teacher)

Page 51

L'heure
The Time

Nom _____

To answer **Quelle heure est-il?** (What is the time?) follow the patterns below. Write the times as indicated.

Il est une heure.
Il est une heure.

Il est deux heures.
Il est deux heures.

Il est minuit.
Il est minuit.

Il est midi.
Il est midi.

Il est cinq heures cinq.
Il est cinq heures cinq.

Il est huit heures un quart.
Il est huit heures un quart.

Page 52

L'heure

Écrivez l'heure de chaque réveil. (Write the times shown on the clocks.)

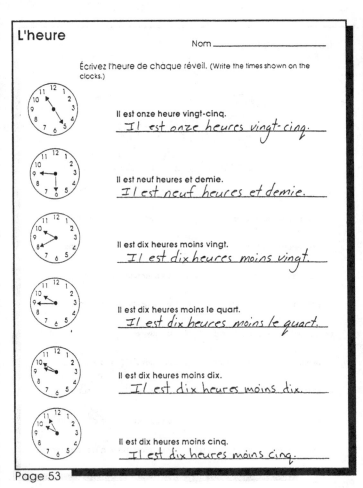

Il est onze heure vingt-cinq.
Il est onze heures vingt-cinq.

Il est neuf heures et demie.
Il est neuf heures et demie.

Il est dix heures moins vingt.
Il est dix heures moins vingt.

Il est dix heures moins le quart.
Il est dix heures moins le quart.

Il est dix heures moins dix.
Il est dix heures moins dix.

Il est dix heures moins cinq.
Il est dix heures moins cinq.

Page 53

L'heure

Écrivez les heures de chaque réveil.

Il est six heures.

Il est onze heures un quart.

Il est une heure et demie.

Il est trois heures moins le quart.

Il est sept heures vingt.

Il est quatre heures moins cinq.

Il est huit heures vingt-cinq.

Page 54

L'heure

À is used to tell **at** what time something will take place.

exemple: À quelle heure est le cours d'espagnol? (At what time is the Spanish class?)

Le cours est à huit heures. (The class is **at** eight o'clock.)

To be more specific about the time use . . .

du matin = in the morning/a.m.

de l'après-midi = in the afternoon/p.m.

du soir = in the evening/p.m.

Regardez l'horaire et répondez aux questions.
(Look at the schedule
and answer the questions.)
Be sure to include a.m. or p.m.

1. À quelle heure est le cours d'anglais?
Le cours d'anglais est à neuf heures du matin

2. À quelle heure est le déjeuner?
Le déjeuner est à onze heures vingt du matin.

3. À quelle heure est le cours de géographie?
Le cours de géographie est à dix heures vingt du

4. À quelle heure est le cours de dessin?
Le cours de dessin est à midi et demi de l'après-

5. À quelle heure est la récréation?
La récréation est à dix heures du matin.

6. À quelle heure est le cours de mathématiques?
Le cours de mathématiques est à une heure et
de l'après-midi

7. À quelle heure est le cours d'histoire?
Le cours d'histoire est à huit heures du matin.

8. À quelle heure finissent les cours?
Les cours finissent à deux heures vingt-cinq de
l'après-midi

Page 55

Les adjectifs possessifs
Possessive Adjectives

One way to indicate possession is to use a noun followed by **de** and the owner's name. Use the masculine form (**du**) or the feminine form (**de la**) with nouns. (There are **no** apostrophes in French.)

la maison **de** Pierre = Pierre's house
le livre **de** Martine = Martine's book

Note: de + le = du

la chaise **du** professeur = the teacher's chair
Tell to whom the following items belong.

1. bedroom/Martine *la chambre de Martine*
2. books/Pierre *les livres de Pierre*
3. bicycle/the boy *la bicyclette du garçon*
4. apartment/the professor *l'apartement du professeur*
5. pencil/the girl *le crayon de la fille*
6. dog/the Proust family *le chien de la famille Proust*

Another way to indicate possession is to use possessive adjectives: my, your, his, her, etc.

	Singular		Plural
	Masculine	Feminine	
my	mon	ma	mes
your (fam.)	ton	ta	tes
your (form. and pl.)	votre	votre	vos
his, her	son	sa	ses
their	leur	leur	leurs
our	notre	notre	nos

Like other adjectives, a possessive adjective must agree in gender and number with the noun it modifies. (Note that the adjective agrees with the **noun** it modifies, not with the owner.)

exemples: mon livre = my book
mes livres = my books

notre chien = our dog
notre maison = our house

nos frères = our brothers
nos soeurs = our sisters

Page 56

Révision

Nom_____

Tell that the following items belong to you.

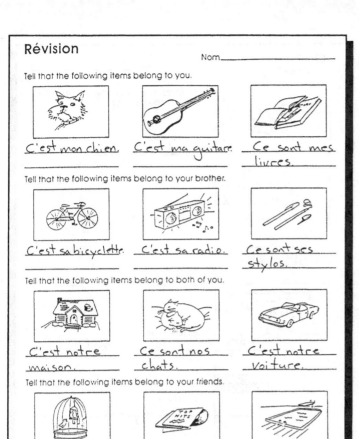

C'est mon chien.   C'est ma guitare.   Ce sont mes livres.

Tell that the following items belong to your brother.

C'est sa bicyclette.   C'est sa radio.   Ce sont ses stylos.

Tell that the following items belong to both of you.

C'est notre maison.   Ce sont nos chats.   C'est notre voiture.

Tell that the following items belong to your friends.

Ce sont leurs oiseaux.   Ce sont leurs disques.   C'est leur piscine.

La curiosité
Curiosity

Nom_____

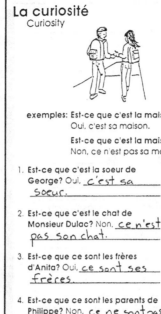

You and a new friend are walking to school. Your friend asks you questions about everything he sees. Answer his questions as indicated.

exemples: Est-ce que c'est la maison d'Emmanuel?
Oui, c'est sa maison.

Est-ce que c'est la maison de Suzanne?
Non, ce n'est pas sa maison.

1. Est-ce que c'est la soeur de George? Oui, c'est sa soeur.

2. Est-ce que c'est le chat de Monsieur Dulac? Non, ce n'est pas son chat.

3. Est-ce que ce sont les frères d'Anita? Oui, ce sont ses frères.

4. Est-ce que ce sont les parents de Philippe? Non, ce ne sont pas ses parents.

5. Est-ce que c'est votre voiture? Oui, c'est ma voiture.

6. Est-ce que c'est notre autobus? Non, ce n'est pas notre autobus.

7. Est-ce que ce sont les livres de Jean et de Michel? Oui, ce sont leurs livres.

8. Est-ce que c'est la classe de Madame Joly? Non, ce n'est pas sa classe.

9. Est-ce que ce sont les chaises des filles? Oui, ce sont leurs chaises.

10. Est-ce que c'est mon lycée? Non, ce n'est pas mon lycée.

11. Est-ce que c'est l'école de ton frère? Oui, c'est son école.

12. Est-ce que ce sont les professeurs de notre lycée? Non, ce ne sont pas nos professeurs.

Allons à . . .
Let's go to . . .

Nom_____

To indicate location use the prepositions à, en, or au meaning "at" or "to." À goes with feminine words, en goes with feminine countries, and au goes with masculine countries and words.

exemples: Elle va en Californie. (She's going to California.—la Californie)
Je vais à la montagne. (I'm going to the mountains.)
Je vais au marché. (I'm going to the market—le marché)

Écrivez où vont les gens.

1. Anita va à la piscine. (swimming pool)

2. Marc va au café. (café)

3. Nous allons à la maison. (house)

4. Les enfants vont au concert. (concert)

5. Je vais à la bibliothèque. (library)

6. Elles vont au cinéma. (movie theatre)

7. Tu vas à la campagne. (country)

8. Vous allez à la banque. (bank)

Quand?
When?

Nom_____

Écrivez les expressions.

aujourd'hui (today) — aujourd'hui

cet après-midi (this afternoon) — cet après-midi

demain (tomorrow) — demain

ce soir (tonight) — ce soir

après les cours (after school) — après les cours

ce week-end (this weekend) — ce week-end

pendant les vacances (during vacation) — pendant les vacances

le week-end prochain (next weekend) — le week-end prochain

ce matin (this morning) — ce matin

la semaine prochaine (next week) — la semaine prochaine

Write in French when you will do the following activities as indicated.

1. mes devoirs (my homework)
mes devoirs, cet après-midi. (this afternoon)

2. aller au lit (go to bed)
aller au lit, ce soir (tonight)

3. se relaxer (relax)
se relaxer, pendant les vacances (during vacation)

4. aller nager (go swimming)
aller nager, le week-end prochain (next week)

5. faire du vélo (ride my bike)
faire du vélo, après les cours (after school)

6. jouer au ballon (play ball)
jouer au ballon, demain (tomorrow)

7. visiter ma grand-mère (visit my grandma)
visiter ma grand-mère, ce week-end (this weekend)

8. manger le petit déjeuner (eat breakfast)
manger le petit déjeuner, ce matin (this morning)

9. aller au cinéma (go to a movie)
aller au cinéma, aujourd'hui (today)

10. aller en voyage (take a trip)
aller en voyage, le week-end prochain (next weekend)

Comment?
How?

Nom _____

Comment, when used with a subject pronoun (je, tu, il, elle, nous, vous, ils, elles), can be used to describe someone.

exemples: **Comment** sont-elles?
        Elles sont tristes.
        Comment est-il?
        Il est riche.

Repondez aux questions.

1. Comment es-tu? (timid) _Je suis timide._

2. Comment êtes-vous? (young) _Je suis jeune._

3. Comment sont-elles? (pessimistic) _Elles sont pessimistes._

4. Comment est-il? (blond) _Il est blond._

5. Comment sont-ils? (polite) _Ils sont polis._

6. Comment est-elle? (nice) _Elle est sympathique._

7. Comment es-tu? (little) _Je suis petit(e)_

8. Comment est-elle? (famous) _Elle est célèbre._

9. Comment êtes-vous? (modest) _Nous sommes modestes._
ou Je suis modeste.

10. Comment sont-ils? (stupid) _Ils sont stupides_

11. Comment sont-elles? (intelligent) _Elles sont intelligente_

12. Comment est-il? (sad) _Il est triste._

Page 61

Où?
Where?

Nom _____

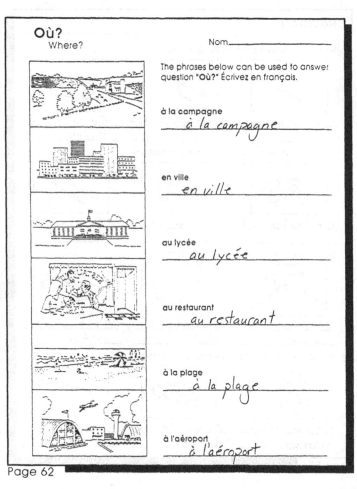

The phrases below can be used to answer question "**Où?**" Écrivez en français.

à la campagne
à la campagne

en ville
en ville

au lycée
au lycée

au restaurant
au restaurant

à la plage
à la plage

à l'aéroport
à l'aéroport

Page 62

Où?

Nom _____

Écrivez les phrases en frança

à la piscine
à la piscine

à la maison
à la maison

au cinéma
au cinéma

au bureau
au bureau

au théatre
au théatre

aux États-Unis
aux États-Unis

Page 63

Où est-ce?
Where is it?

Nom _____

exemple: **C'est près de Marie.** (It's near Marie.)

Écrivez en français.

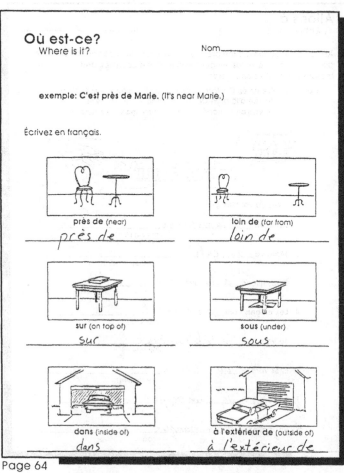

près de (near)
près de

loin de (far from)
loin de

sur (on top of)
sur

sous (under)
sous

dans (inside of)
dans

à l'extérieur de (outside of)
à l'extérieur de

Page 64

Où est-ce?

Nom _____

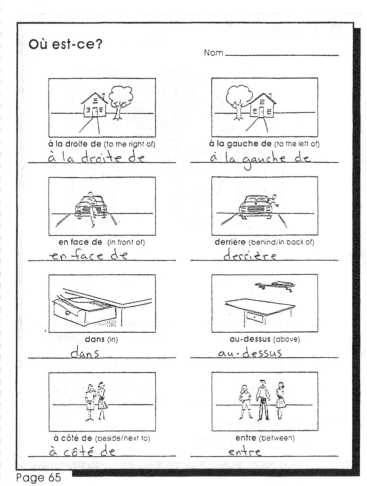

à la droite de (to the right of)
à la droite de

à la gauche de (to the left of)
à la gauche de

en face de (in front of)
en face de

derrière (behind/in back of)
derrière

dans (in)
dans

au-dessus (above)
au-dessus

à côté de (beside/next to)
à côté de

entre (between)
entre

Page 65

Où est-ce?

Answers vary

Nom _____

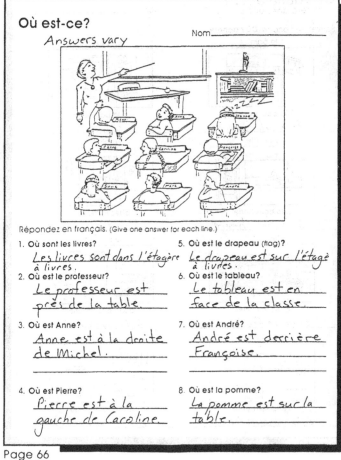

Répondez en français. (Give one answer for each line.)

1. Où sont les livres?
   Les livres sont dans l'étagère à livres.
2. Où est le professeur?
   Le professeur est près de la table.
3. Où est Anne?
   Anne est à la droite de Michel.
4. Où est Pierre?
   Pierre est à la gauche de Caroline.
5. Où est le drapeau (flag)?
   Le drapeau est sur l'étagè à livres.
6. Où est le tableau?
   Le tableau est en face de la classe.
7. Où est André?
   André est derrière Françoise.
8. Où est la pomme?
   La pomme est sur la table.

Page 66

Où?

Nom _____

Answer the questions according to the pictures.

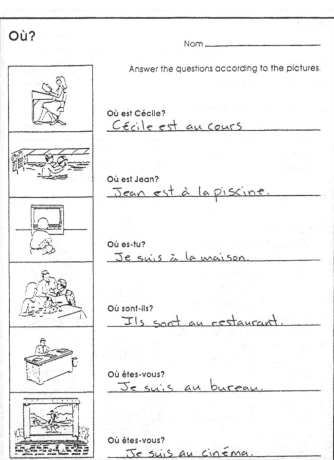

Où est Cécile?
Cécile est au cours

Où est Jean?
Jean est à la piscine.

Où es-tu?
Je suis à la maison.

Où sont-ils?
Ils sont au restaurant.

Où êtes-vous?
Je suis au bureau.

Où êtes-vous?
Je suis au cinéma.

Page 67

Où?

Nom _____

Answer the questions according to the pictures.

Où nagent Georges et Françoise?
Ils nagent à la plage.

Où travaille Martine?
Elle travaille au bureau.

Où sont les gens?
Ils sont en ville.

Où étudies-tu?
J'étudie à la maison.

Où sont les acteurs?
Ils sont au théatre.

Où est l'avion?
L'avion est à l'aéroport

Page 68

Où s'achète . . . ?
Where does one buy . . . ?

Nom_____

Écrivez en français. **Où s'achète . . .**

le pain?

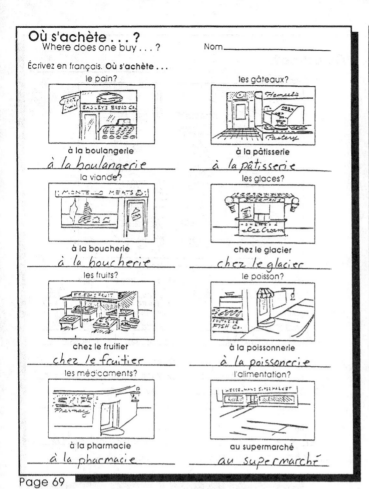

à la boulangerie
à la boulangerie

les gâteaux?

à la pâtisserie
à la pâtisserie

la viande?

à la boucherie
à la boucherie

les glaces?

chez le glacier
chez le glacier

les fruits?

chez le fruitier
chez le fruitier

le poisson?

à la poissonnerie
à la poissonnerie

les médicaments?

à la pharmacie
à la pharmacie

l'alimentation?

au supermarché
au supermarché

Où s'achète . . . ?

Nom_____

Répondez en français.

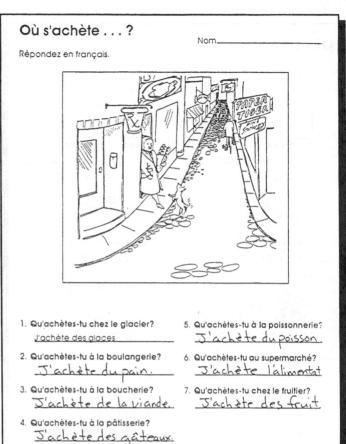

1. Qu'achètes-tu chez le glacier?
   J'achète des glaces.

2. Qu'achètes-tu à la boulangerie?
   J'achète du pain.

3. Qu'achètes-tu à la boucherie?
   J'achète de la viande.

4. Qu'achètes-tu à la pâtisserie?
   J'achète des gâteaux.

5. Qu'achètes-tu à la poissonnerie?
   J'achète du poisson.

6. Qu'achètes-tu au supermarché?
   J'achète l'alimentat

7. Qu'achètes-tu chez le fruitier?
   J'achète des fruit

Vocabulaire
Vocabulary

Nom_____

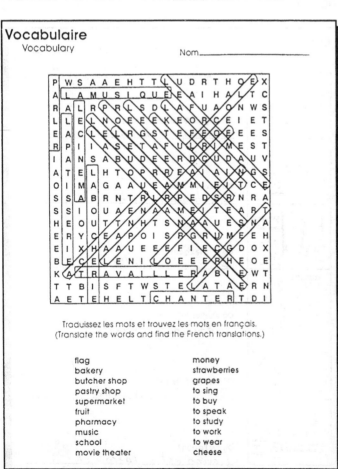

Traduisez les mots et trouvez les mots en français.
(Translate the words and find the French translations.)

flag	money
bakery	strawberries
butcher shop	grapes
pastry shop	to sing
supermarket	to buy
fruit	to speak
pharmacy	to study
music	to work
school	to wear
movie theater	cheese

Aller
To go

Nom_____

Aller (to go) is an irregular verb.

Aller is usually followed by à (to).

Some places you might go are . . .

	Aller		
je	vais	nous	allon
tu	vas	vous	allez
il	va	ils	vont
elle	va	elles	vont

la bibliotèque	= the library		
le café	= the café		
le musée	= the museum	**le parc**	= the park
le lycée	= the school	**l'hotel**	= the hotel
		la gare	= the train station

Answer the following questions using aller à and the place in the picture.

1. Où vas-tu?
   Je vais au lycée.

2. Où va Laurence?
   Il va au parc.

3. Où vont Jean et Christophe?
   Ils vont à la plage

4. Où allez-vous?
   Nous allons à la gare.

5. Où vont les touristes?
   Ils vont à l'hôtel.

6. Où allez-vous?
   Nous allons au café.

7. Où va Jean-Luc?
   Il va à l'aéroport.

8. Où va Pascale?
   Pascale va au théatre.

Aller

Nom _____

Aller is followed by **an infinitive** to tell what is going to happen in the future.

exemple: Je vais voyager demain. (I'm going to travel tomorrow.)

Tell what the following people are going to do tomorrow by combining the given elements.

exemple: Pierre/travailler

<u>Pierre va travailler demain.</u>

1. Cécile/chanter <u>Cecile va chanter demain.</u>
2. Christine et Anne/danser <u>Christine et Anne vont danser demain.</u>
3. Les enfants/étudier <u>Les enfants vont étudier demain.</u>
4. Je/marcher <u>Je vais marcher demain.</u>
5. Nous/répondre <u>Nous allons répondre demain.</u>
6. Les soeurs/visiter <u>Les soeurs vont visiter demain.</u>
7. Emmanuel/travailler <u>Emmanuel va travailler demain.</u>

If you make a sentence with two verbs negative, be sure to put **ne** before the first verb and **pas** after the first verb..

exemple: Non, je ne vais **pas** chanter. (No. I'm not going to sing.)

Répondez aux questions en français.

1. Vas-tu étudier demain? Oui, <u>je vais étudier demain.</u>
2. Allez-vous manger ce soir? Oui, <u>je vais manger ce soir.</u>
3. Allez-vous parler en classe? Non, <u>je ne vais pas parler en classe.</u>
4. Va-t-elle écouter? Oui, <u>elle va écouter.</u>
5. Va-t-il regarder la télévision? Non, <u>il ne va pas regarder la télévision.</u>
6. Allez-vous acheter des vêtements? Non, <u>nous n'allons pas acheter des vêtements.</u>
7. Vas-tu nager demain? Oui, <u>je vais nager demain.</u>

Page 73

L'impératif
The Imperative

Nom _____

When you tell someone to do something you use the command form of a verb, the **imperative** (l'impératif).

To give a command to someone you know well using a regular verb, use the **tu** form of the verb minus the -s. As in English, the "you" (tu) is understood.

exemple: Tu danses. (You dance/are dancing.)

Danse! (Dance!)

Tell your friend to do the following things:

Sing! <u>Chantes!</u>
Speak French! <u>Parles français!</u>
Watch TV! <u>Regardes la télévision!</u>
Swim! <u>Nages!</u>
Eat! <u>Manges!</u>
Listen! <u>Écoutes!</u>
Study! <u>Étudies!</u>
Cook! <u>Cuisines!</u>

To give a command to someone you address in a formal way, use the formal form without the pronoun.

exemple: Vous dansez. (You dance/are dancing.)

Dansez! (Dance!)

To practice, tell your older neighbor to do the following things:

Sing! <u>Chantez</u>   Eat! <u>Mangez!</u>
Speak French! <u>Parlez français!</u> Listen! <u>Écoutez!</u>
Watch TV! <u>Regardez la télévision!</u> Study! <u>Étudiez!</u>
Swim! <u>Nagez!</u>   Cook! <u>Cuisinez!</u>

Page 74

L'impératif

Nom _____

The command form for **nous** (Let's dance!, Let's sing!) is the same as the conjugated form of the verb for **nous**. The subject pronoun (nous) is omitted since it is understood.

exemples: Dansons!   Let's dance!
         Chantons!   Let's sing!
         Parlons!   Lets talk!

Écrivez l'impératif. Write the imperative form of the verb.

1. Eat! (vous) <u>Mangez!</u>
2. Jump! (vous) <u>Sautez!</u>
3. Sing! (tu) <u>Chantes!</u>
4. Let's dance! <u>Dansons!</u>
5. Dance! (vous) <u>Dansez!</u>

6. Let's work! <u>Travaillons!</u>
7. Look! (tu) <u>Regardes!</u>
8. Sing! (vous) <u>Chantez!</u>
9. Let's look! <u>Regardons!</u>
10. Jump! (tu) <u>Sautes!</u>

11. Dance! (tu) <u>Danses!</u>
12. Listen! (vous) <u>Écoutez!</u>
13. Work! (vous) <u>Travaillez!</u>
14. Look! (vous) <u>Regardez!</u>

Page 75

Avoir
To have

Nom _____

Avoir (to have) is an important irregular verb.

Avoir is usually followed by a noun.

exemple: J'ai une radio.

Avoir			
j' (je)	ai	nous	avons
tu	as	vous	avez
il	a	ils	ont
elle	a	elles	ont

Using the pictures, tell what the following people have.

la guitare

1. Marc <u>a une guitare</u>
2. Je <u>J'ai des disques.</u>
3. Anne <u>a un crayon.</u>
4. Nous <u>avons des livres.</u>
5. Elle <u>a du popcorn.</u>
6. <u>Qu'est-ce qu'avez-</u> vous (sing.)?
7. Ils <u>ont des chiens</u>
8. <u>Qu'est-ce qu'avez-</u> vous (pl.)?
9. Tu <u>as une bicyclette.</u>
10. Nous <u>avons une pomme.</u>
11. Elles <u>ont des chaussures.</u>
12. Monsieur Dulac <u>a une voiture.</u>

les disques

la maison

les livres

le crayon

le popcorn

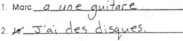
les chiens

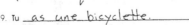
le papier

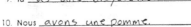
la bicyclette

la pomme

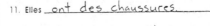
les chaussures

la voitur

Page 76

---

    121   IF 8793 French

À la maison
At home

Écrivez les mots en français.

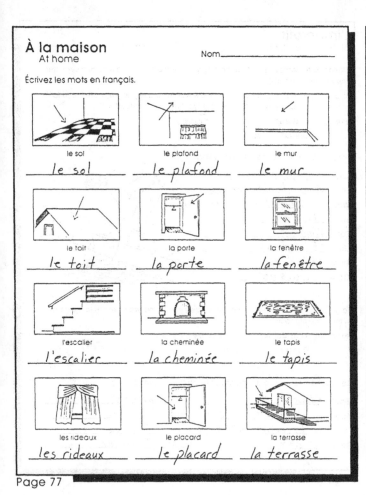

le sol	le plafond	le mur
le sol	*le plafond*	*le mur*
le toit	la porte	la fenêtre
le toit	*la porte*	*la fenêtre*
l'escalier	la cheminée	le tapis
l'escalier	*la cheminée*	*le tapis*
les rideaux	le placard	la terrasse
les rideaux	*le placard*	*la terrasse*

À la maison

Écrivez les mots en français.

la cuisine	la chambre
la cuisine	*la chambre*
la salle à manger	le salon
la salle à manger	*le salon*
la salle de bain	le jardin
la salle de bain	*le jardin*

La famille Dulac

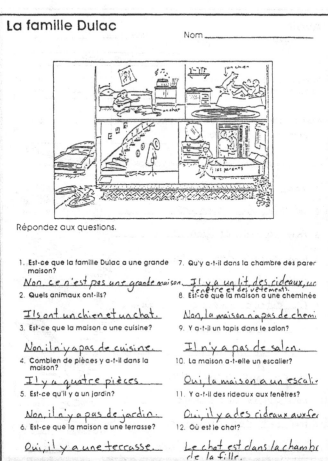

Répondez aux questions.

1. Est-ce que la famille Dulac a une grande maison?
   Non, ce n'est pas une grande maison.

2. Quels animaux ont-ils?
   Ils ont un chien et un chat.

3. Est-ce que la maison a une cuisine?
   Non, il n'y a pas de cuisine.

4. Combien de pièces y a-t-il dans la maison?
   Il y a quatre pièces.

5. Est-ce qu'il y a un jardin?
   Non, il n'y a pas de jardin.

6. Est-ce que la maison a une terrasse?
   Oui, il y a une terrasse.

7. Qu'y a-t-il dans la chambre des parer
   Il y a un lit, des rideaux, u fenêtre et des vêtements.

8. Est-ce que la maison a une cheminée
   Non, la maison n'a pas de chemi

9. Y a-t-il un tapis dans le salon?
   Il n'y a pas de salon.

10. La maison a-t-elle un escalier?
    Oui, la maison a un escali

11. Y a-t-il des rideaux aux fenêtres?
    Oui, il y a des rideaux aux fe

12. Où est le chat?
    Le chat est dans la chamb de la fille.

La cuisine

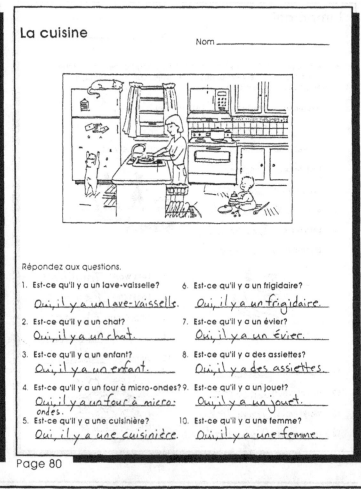

Répondez aux questions.

1. Est-ce qu'il y a un lave-vaisselle?
   Oui, il y a un lave-vaisselle.

2. Est-ce qu'il y a un chat?
   Oui, il y a un chat.

3. Est-ce qu'il y a un enfant?
   Oui, il y a un enfant.

4. Est-ce qu'il y a un four à micro-ondes?
   Oui, il y a un four à micro-ondes.

5. Est-ce qu'il y a une cuisinière?
   Oui, il y a une cuisinière.

6. Est-ce qu'il y a un frigidaire?
   Oui, il y a un frigidaire.

7. Est-ce qu'il y a un évier?
   Oui, il y a un évier.

8. Est-ce qu'il y a des assiettes?
   Oui, il y a des assiettes.

9. Est-ce qu'il y a un jouet?
   Oui, il y a un jouet.

10. Est-ce qu'il y a une femme?
    Oui, il y a une femme.

L'âge
Age

Nom_____

The verb **avoir** is used to talk about age.

Quel âge as-tu? (How old are you?)

J'ai quatorze ans. (I'm 14 years old.)

Ask how old the subjects are in parentheses and respond using the numbers indicated. Use the pattern: subject + avoir + number + ans

exemple: (elle) <u>Quel âge a-t-elle?</u>

(30) <u>Elle a trente ans.</u>

1. (tu) <u>Quel âge as-tu?</u>
   (15) <u>J'ai quinze ans.</u>
2. (vous) <u>Quel âge avez-vous?</u>
   (10) <u>J'ai dix ans.</u>
3. (il) <u>Quel âge a-t-il?</u>
   (21) <u>Il a vingt et un ans.</u>
4. (vous) <u>Quel âge avez-vous?</u>
   (80) <u>J'ai quatre-vingt ans.</u>
5. (Monique) <u>Quel âge a Monique?</u>
   (13) <u>Elle a treize ans.</u>
6. (l'enfant) <u>Quel âge a l'enfant.</u>
   (1) <u>Il a un an.</u>
7. (tu) <u>Quel âge as-tu?</u>
   (4) <u>J'ai quatre ans.</u>
8. (elles) <u>Quels âges ont-elles?</u>
   (18) <u>Elles ont dix-huit ans.</u>
9. (Madame Dulac) <u>Quel âge a Madame Dulac?</u>
   (95) <u>Madame Dulac a quatre-vingt-quinze</u>
10. (Françoise et David) <u>Quels âges ont Françoise et David</u>
    (40) <u>Françoise et David ont quarante ans.</u>

La faim et la soif
Hunger and Thirst

Nom_____

The verb **avoir** is also used when you are talking about **hunger** and **thirst**.

avoir faim. = to be hungry
J'ai faim. = I am hungry.
avoir soif. = to be thirsty
Il a soif. = He is thirsty.

State that the following people are hungry or thirsty as indicated.

1. Nous/faim
   <u>Nous avons faim.</u>
2. Elles/soif
   <u>Elles ont soif.</u>
3. Tu/faim
   <u>Tu as faim.</u>
4. Elle/soif
   <u>Elle a soif.</u>
5. Vous/faim
   <u>Vous avez faim.</u>

Répondez aux questions.

1. Est-ce que Georges a soif?
   <u>Oui, Georges a soif.</u>
2. As-tu faim?
   <u>Oui, j'ai faim.</u>
3. Est-ce que Monsieur Dulac a très faim?
   <u>Oui, Monsieur Dulac a très faim.</u>
4. Avez-vous très soif?
   <u>Non, je n'ai pas très soif.</u>
5. Est-ce que Colette a soif?
   <u>Non, Colette n'a pas soif.</u>
6. Avez-vous très soif?
   <u>Oui, j'ai très soif.</u>
7. Est-ce que les enfants ont faim?
   <u>Non, les enfants n'ont pas faim.</u>

Le chaud et le froid
Hot and Cold

Nom_____

Another set of expressions using **avoir** are:

avoir chaud = to be hot/to feel hot   **avoir froid** = to be cold/to feel col

Tell how the following people would feel according to the temperature.

1. je/90°F
   <u>J'ai chaud.</u>
2. elle/10°F
   <u>Elle a froid.</u>
3. nous/40°F
   <u>Nous avons froid.</u>
4. tu/86°F
   <u>Tu as chaud.</u>
5. vous/0°F
   <u>Vous avez froid.</u>

Tell how the following people feel based on how they are dressed.

1. Emmanuel porte un manteau.
   <u>Emmanuel a froid.</u>
2. Madame Dulac est en maillot de bain.
   <u>Madame Dulac a chaud.</u>
3. Je porte un pullover et un pantalon.
   <u>J'ai froid.</u>
4. Vous portez un short et une chemise.
   <u>Vous avez chaud.</u>

Note: In France the Celsius temperature is used.

Can you tell how these people feel using the centigrade thermometer?

1. Elles/5°C
   <u>Elles ont froid.</u>
2. Il/30°C
   <u>Il a chaud.</u>

Faire
To do

Nom_____

Faire is an important irregular verb. It is used in many expressions.

It means to do or to make.

Faire			
je	fais	nous	faisons
tu	fais	vous	faites
il	fait	ils	font
elle	fait	elles	font

exemple:

Que fais-tu? (What are you doing./What do you do?)
Je fais mes devoirs. (I'm doing homework./I do homework.)

Expressions using faire:

faire ses devoirs = to do homework
faire des projets = to make plans
faire un picnic = to have a picnic
faire la fête = to have a party
faire un barbecue = to have a barbeque
faire sa valise = to pack your suitcase

Que font-ils?

Ils <u>font la fête.</u> Elle <u>fait sa valise.</u> Emmanuel <u>fait ses devoirs.</u>

Vous <u>faites un picnic.</u> Je <u>fais un barbecue.</u> Tu <u>fais des projets.</u>

       IF 8793 French

Le temps
The Weather

Nom _____

Faire is also used in some expressions to talk about the weather.

Quel temps fait-il? (What's the weather like?)

Écrivez en français.

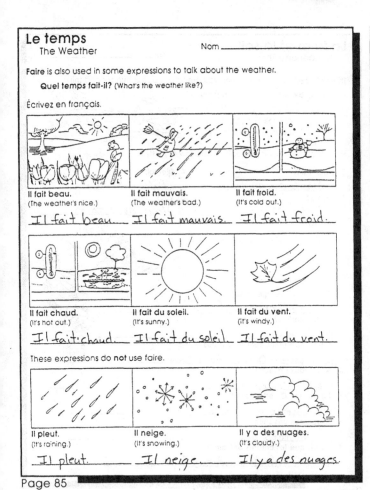

Il fait beau.
(The weather's nice.)

Il fait beau.

Il fait mauvais.
(The weather's bad.)

Il fait mauvais.

Il fait froid.
(It's cold out.)

Il fait froid.

Il fait chaud.
(It's hot out.)

Il fait chaud.

Il fait du soleil.
(It's sunny.)

Il fait du soleil.

Il fait du vent.
(It's windy.)

Il fait du vent.

These expressions do **not** use faire.

Il pleut.
(It's raining.)

Il pleut.

Il neige.
(It's snowing.)

Il neige.

Il y a des nuages.
(It's cloudy.)

Il y a des nuages.

Page 85

Quel temps fait-il sur les photos?

Nom _____

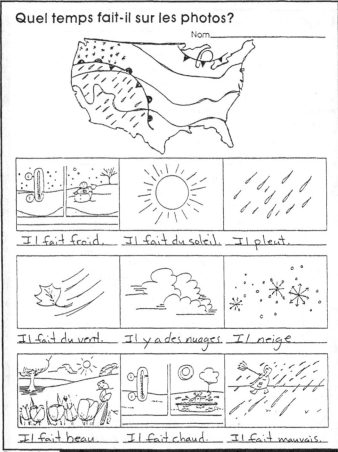

Il fait froid.   _Il fait du soleil._   _Il pleut._

Il fait du vent.   _Il y a des nuages._   _Il neige._

Il fait beau.   _Il fait chaud._   _Il fait mauvais._

Page 86

Les saisons
The Seasons

Nom _____

Écrivez en français.

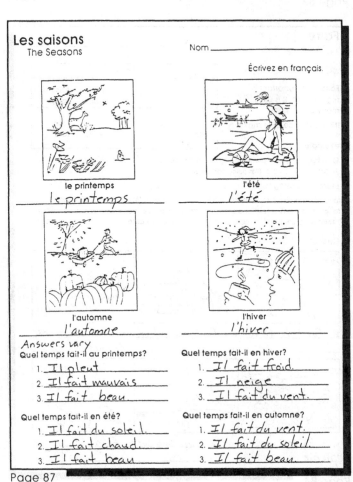

le printemps
le printemps

l'été
l'été

l'automne
l'automne

l'hiver
l'hiver

Answers vary

Quel temps fait-il au printemps?
1. _Il pleut_
2. _Il fait mauvais_
3. _Il fait beau_

Quel temps fait-il en hiver?
1. _Il fait froid._
2. _Il neige._
3. _Il fait du vent._

Quel temps fait-il en été?
1. _Il fait du soleil._
2. _Il fait chaud._
3. _Il fait beau_

Quel temps fait-il en automne?
1. _Il fait du vent._
2. _Il fait du soleil._
3. _Il fait beau._

Page 87

Les sports
Sports

Nom _____

Jouer is a verb used to talk about sports. It means to play.

exemples: Elle **joue** au volley-ball.

Ils **jouent** au football.

Écrivez en français.

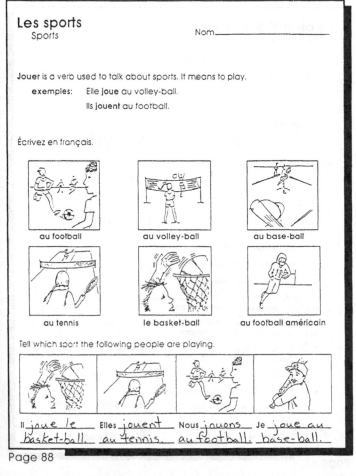

au football   au volley-ball   au base-ball

au tennis   le basket-ball   au football américain

Tell which sport the following people are playing.

Il _joue le basket-ball._   Elles _jouent au tennis._   Nous _jouons au football._   Je _joue au base-ball._

Page 88

Pour pratiquer les sports
To Practice Sports

Nom_____

Here are some objects we use to play various sports. Écrivez en français.

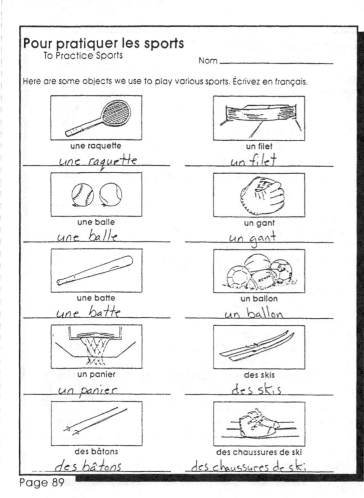

une raquette
une raquette

un filet
un filet

une balle
une balle

un gant
un gant

une batte
une batte

un ballon
un ballon

un panier
un panier

des skis
des skis

des bâtons
des bâtons

des chaussures de ski
des chaussures de ski

Page 89

Pour pratiquer les sports

Nom_____

Tell which items are necessary to participate in each sport shown.

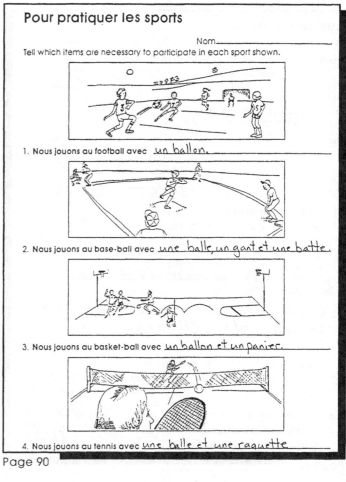

1. Nous jouons au football avec _un ballon._

2. Nous jouons au base-ball avec _une balle, un gant et une batte._

3. Nous jouons au basket-ball avec _un ballon et un panier._

4. Nous jouons au tennis avec _une balle et une raquette_

Page 90

Les comparaisons
Comparisons

Nom_____

To compare two things or people in French use the following:

plus + adjective + que.
(more _____ than)

exemple: Antoine est plus grand que Paul.
(Antoine is taller than Paul.)

Note: Remember that adjectives must agree in gender and number with the nouns they modify.

exemples: Anne est plus grande que Marie.

Les voitures sont plus grandes que les bicyclettes.

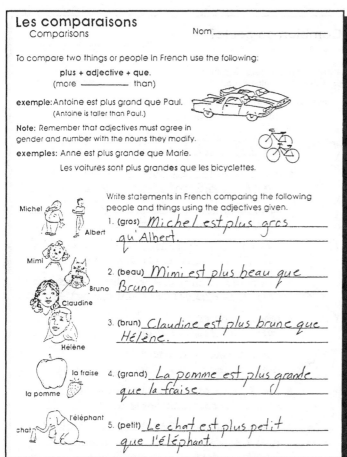

Write statements in French comparing the following people and things using the adjectives given.

1. (gros) _Michel est plus gros qu'Albert._

2. (beau) _Mimi est plus beau que Bruno._

3. (brun) _Claudine est plus brune que Hélène._

4. (grand) _La pomme est plus grande que la fraise._

5. (petit) _Le chat est plus petit que l'éléphant._

Page 91

Les comparaisons

Nom_____

Another way to compare two people or things is to use:

moins + adjective + que.
(less _____ than)

exemples: Paul est **moins** grand qu'Antoine.
(Paul is less tall than Antoine.)

Anne est moins grande que Marie.

Write statements in French comparing the following people and things using **moins/que.**

1. (grand) _La bicyclette est moins grande que la voiture._

2. (sympathique) _Paul est moins sympathique que Robert._

3. (intéressant) _La télévision est moins intéressant que le film._

4. (intelligent) _Catherine est moins intelligente qu'Estèle_

5. (grand) _Les filles sont moins grands que les garçons._

6. (gros) _Les girafes sont moins gros que les cochons._

Page 92

IF 8793 French

Les comparaisons

Nom_____

You can compare things that are equal by using the expression:

aussi + adjective + que

(as _____ as)

exemple: L'espagnol est **aussi** important **que** l'anglais.
(Spanish is as important as English.)

Tell that the two people or items mentioned are equal in the given quality.

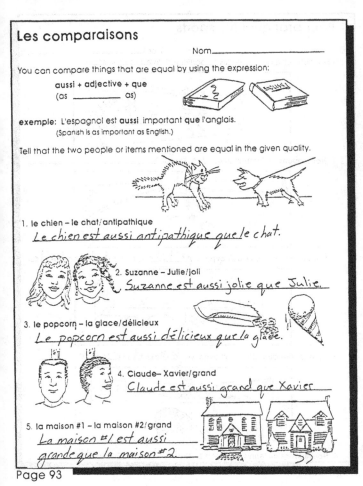

1. le chien – le chat/antipathique

Le chien est aussi antipathique que le chat.

2. Suzanne – Julie/joli

Suzanne est aussi jolie que Julie.

3. le popcorn – la glace/délicieux

Le popcorn est aussi délicieux que la glace.

4. Claude – Xavier/grand

Claude est aussi grand que Xavier.

5. la maison #1 – la maison #2/grand

La maison #1 est aussi grande que la maison #2.

Les comparaisons – pratique

Nom_____

Practice all three types of comparisons by writing the following sentences in French.

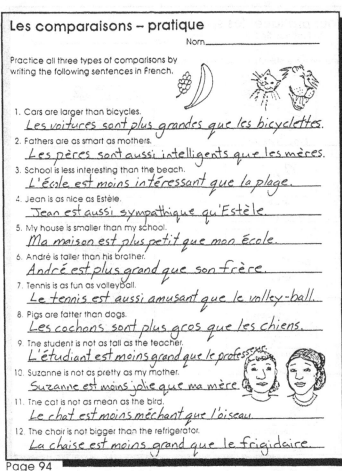

1. Cars are larger than bicycles.
Les voitures sont plus grandes que les bicyclettes.

2. Fathers are as smart as mothers.
Les pères sont aussi intelligents que les mères.

3. School is less interesting than the beach.
L'école est moins intéressant que la plage.

4. Jean is as nice as Estèle.
Jean est aussi sympathique qu'Estèle.

5. My house is smaller than my school.
Ma maison est plus petit que mon école.

6. André is taller than his brother.
André est plus grand que son frère.

7. Tennis is as fun as volleyball.
Le tennis est aussi amusant que le volley-ball.

8. Pigs are fatter than dogs.
Les cochons sont plus gros que les chiens.

9. The student is not as tall as the teacher.
L'étudiant est moins grand que le professeur.

10. Suzanne is not as pretty as my mother.
Suzanne est moins jolie que ma mère.

11. The cat is not as mean as the bird.
Le chat est moins méchant que l'oiseau.

12. The chair is not bigger than the refrigerator.
La chaise est moins grand que le frigidaire.

Combien ça coûte?
How much does it cost?

Nom_____

To ask how much something costs, the verb **coûter** is used with the question words **Combien ça . . .** You will only use two forms of the verb **coûter; coûte** (it costs) and **coûtent** (they cost).

exemples: Le livre coûte trente francs.
Deux livres coûtent soixante francs.

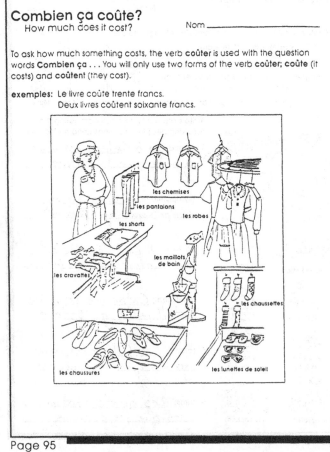

Combien ça coûte?

Nom_____

A sale is on at your favorite clothing store. Ask the salesperson how much each item in parentheses costs. Then write the response using the given price.

exemple: (socks) Combien coûtent les chaussettes?
(10 F.) Elles coûtent dix francs.

1. (shorts) Combien coûtent les shorts.
(30 F.) Les shorts coûtent trente francs.

2. (ties) Combien coûtent les cravattes?
(20 F.) Elles coûtent vingt francs.

3. (dress) Combien coûte la robe?
(100 F.) Elle coûte cent francs.

4. (swimsuit) Combien coûte le maillot de bain?
(70 F.) Il coûte soixante-dix francs.

5. (sunglasses) Combien coûtent les lunettes de soleil
(20 F.) Les lunettes de soleil coûtent vingt francs.

6. (shoes) Combien coûtent les chaussures?
(40 F.) Elles coûtent quarante francs.

7. (pants) Combien coûtent les pantalons?
(80 F.) Les pantalons coûtent quatre-vingt francs

8. (shirt) Combien coûte la chemise?
(60 F.) Elle coûte soixante francs.

9. (socks) Combien coûtent les chaussettes?
(10 F.) Les chaussettes coûtent dix francs.

D'où viens-tu?
Where do you come from?

Nom_____

Venir			
je	viens	nous	venons
tu	viens	vous	venez
il	vient	ils	viennent
elle	vient	elles	viennent

The verb **venir** (to come) is irregular.

exemples: D'où viens-tu?
(Where do you come from?)

Je viens de la Bolivie.
(I come from Bolivia.)

Use the verb **parler** (to speak) with the name of the language spoken.

exemple: Je parle français. (I speak French.)

Using the verb **venir**, tell where the following people come from and what language they speak.

1. Claude _vient_ du Mexique.
   Il parle _espagnol_.

2. Les filles _viennent_ de France.
   Elles parlent _français_.

3. Nous _venons_ du Japon.
   Nous parlons _japonais_.

4. Françoise et Marcel _viennent_ d'Italie.
   Ils parlent _italien_.

5. Vous _venez_ de Russie.
   Vous parlez _russe_.

6. Je _viens_ d'Allemagne.
   Je parle _allemand_.

7. Anne _vient_ du Portugal.
   Elle parle _portugais_.

8. Tu _viens_ d'Angleterre.
   Tu parles _anglais_.

Languages Spoken Around the World	
l'espagnol	= Spanish
l'anglais	= English
le français	= French
l'allemand	= German
le russe	= Russian
le portugais	= Portuguese
l'italien	= Italian
le japonais	= Japanese
le chinois	= Chinese

Il y a
There Is/There Are

Nom_____

Il y a is an expression meaning "there is" or "there are." It can be followed by a singular or a plural noun.

Qu'y a-t-il dans le réfrigérateur? (What is there in the refrigerator?)
Il y a du lait dans le réfrigérateur. (There's milk in the refrigerator.)

Combien d'enfants y a-t-il dans la classe? (How many children are there in the class?)
Il y a douze enfants dans la classe. (There are twelve children in the class.)

Combien de maisons y a-t-il dans la rue? (How many houses are there on the street?)
Il y a vingt maisons dans la rue. (There are twenty houses on the street.)

Note: Since **il y a** is a verbal expression, write **il n'y a pas** to make it negative.

Il n'y a pas de livres ici. (There are no books here./ There aren't any books here.)

Regardez les photos et écrivez les réponses.

1. Combien de garçons y a-t-il dans la famille?
   Il y a trois garçons dans la famille
2. Combien de filles y a-t-il dans la famille?
   Il n'y a pas de filles dans la famille.
3. Y a-t-il un père?
   Oui, il y a un père.
4. Y a-t-il une mère?
   Oui, il y a une mère.

1. Y a-t-il des chiens?
   Oui, il y a des chiens.
2. Combien de chiens y a-t-il?
   Il y a trois chiens.
3. Combien de chats y a-t-il?
   Il y a deux chats.
4. Combien d'oiseaux y a-t-il?
   Il y a deux oiseaux.

Monique et Claude

Nom_____

Lisez les paragraphes et répondez aux questions.

Bonjour! Je m'apelle Monique Dulac. Je viens de France. Je suis l'amie de Claude Pelletier.

Claude vient des États-Unis. Il est formidable. Il est petit, blond, et franc. Il aime faire du sport. Moi aussi. Nous aimons le tennis et le foot-ball. Nous n'aimons pas nager ou courir.

Je suis étudiante dans un lycée de Dijon. Claude est étudiant dans un lycée de Lyons. J'aime l'histoire et surtout les mathématiques. Claude n'aime pas les mathématiques mais il aime l'histoire aussi. Nous sommes intelligents.

1. Est-ce que Monique vient des États-Unis?
   Non, Monique ne vient pas des États-Unis.
2. Est-ce que Claude vient d'Espagne?
   Non, Claude ne vient pas d'Espagne.
3. Comment est Claude?
   Claude est petit, blond, franc et formidable.
4. Est-ce que Claude aime faire du sport?
   Oui, il aime faire du sport.
5. Est-ce que Monique aime faire du sport aussi?
   Oui, Monique aime faire du sport aussi.
6. Est-ce qu'ils aiment courrir?
   Non, ils n'aiment pas courrir.
7. Où est le lycée de Monique?
   Monique est étudiante dans un lycée de Dijon.
8. Où est le lycée de Claude?
   Claude est étudiant dans un lycée de Lyons.
9. Est-ce que Monique aime les mathématiques?
   Oui, elle aime les mathématiques
10. Sont-ils intelligents?
    Oui, ils sont intelligents.

Anita

Nom_____

Lisez les paragraphes et répondez aux questions. (Read the paragraphs and answer the questions.)

Anita vit à Santiago. Elle vient du Chili. Elle parle espagnol et français aussi. Elle aime le cours d'anglais au lycée. Elle est très intelligente mais elle n'aime pas le professeur de biologie. Elle aime porter une chemisette et un blue-jean au lycée. Elle aime chanter et danser.

1. Où vit Anita?
   Anita vit à Santiago.
2. Est-ce que Anita vient du Méxique?
   Non, Anita ne vient pas du Méxique.
3. Quelles classes plaisent à Anita?
   Anita aime le cours d'anglais.
4. Est-ce qu'elle aime aller au lycée?
   Oui, elle aime aller au lycée.
5. Parle-t-elle français?
   Oui, elle parle français.

Paul

Paul est très sportif. Il aime le football. Il est grand, blond et en pleine forme. Il vit à la campagne. Il travaille avec son oncle. Il aime la campagne. Il n'aime pas le lycée, les cours ou les professeurs. Il aime les étudiantes et, surtout, les jolies filles. Paul et ses amis écoutent la radio et regardent la télévision.

1. Est-ce que Paul est sportif?
   Oui, Paul est sportif.
2. Est-ce que Paul est petit et brun?
   Non, Paul n'est pas petit et brun.
3. Où vit Paul?
   Paul vit à la campagne.
4. Est-ce qu'il étudie à la campagne?
   Non, il n'étudie pas à la campagne.
5. Est-ce qu'il aime le lycée?
   Non, il n'aime pas le lycée.

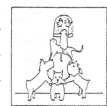

 IF 8793 French

Vocabulaire
Vocabulary   Nom_____

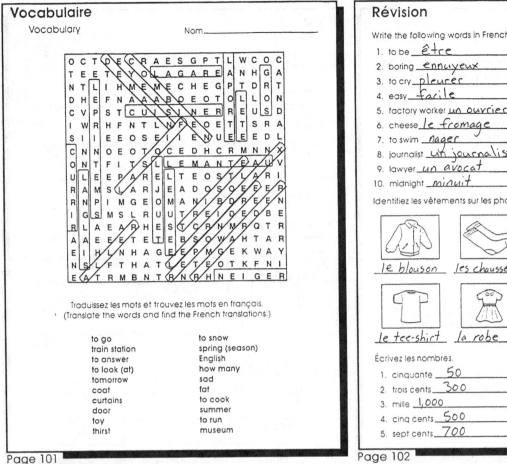

Traduissez les mots et trouvez les mots en français.
(Translate the words and find the French translations.)

to go	to snow
train station	spring (season)
to answer	English
to look (at)	how many
tomorrow	sad
coat	fat
curtains	to cook
door	summer
toy	to run
thirst	museum

Révision
Nom_____

Write the following words in French.

1. to be _être_
2. boring _ennuyeux_
3. to cry _pleurer_
4. easy _facile_
5. factory worker _un ouvrier_
6. cheese _le fromage_
7. to swim _nager_
8. journalist _un journaliste_
9. lawyer _un avocat_
10. midnight _minuit_
11. nurse _l'infirmière_
12. to play _jouer_
13. to read _lire_
14. sad _triste_
15. sandals _les sandales_
16. shoes _les chaussures_
17. sixty _soixante_
18. tie _la cravate_
19. what _que... or commen'_
20. to work _travailler_

Identifiez les vêtements sur les photos.

le blouson   _les chaussettes_   _les chaussures_   _le pullover_

le tee-shirt   _la robe_   _le short_   _le maillot de ba_

Écrivez les nombres.

1. cinquante _50_
2. trois cents _300_
3. mille _1,000_
4. cinq cents _500_
5. sept cents _700_
6. soixante-douze _72_
7. quatre-vingt onze _91_
8. un million _1,000,000_
9. quatre mille _4,000_
10. soixante _60_

To use the book . . .

a. Read each title and its meaning.

b. Read all directions.

c. Look at each picture (where appropriate) and follow the directions for each activity.

d. Review many of the concepts by completing the various exercises and puzzles included in the book.

e. Use the answer key to check your work.

Credits . . .

Adapted and Translated by: Danielle de Gregory
Adapted from *Spanish Middle/High School* (IF 8791) **by:** Rose Thomas
Cover Illustration: Gary Hoover
Inside Illustration: Kristina VanOss
Project Director/Editor: Danielle de Gregory
Art Production: Darcy Bell-Myers
French Consultant: Martine Nagy-Skovbroten